SOCIAL DEMAND

AND HOW TO PROVIDE FOR IT

Brian Ellis is Emeritus Professor at La Trobe University, and Professorial Fellow in Philosophy at the University of Melbourne. He has published widely in books and articles on philosophy of science, logic and metaphysics, and was the Editor of the Australasian Journal of Philosophy for twelve years. In 1994, Ellis retired from La Trobe, and has since published four more books, including Social Humanism: A New Metaphysics, (Routledge, 2012), which concerns the philosophical foundations of the welfare state. In this essay, Ellis develops a new and more vital philosophy for Labor—one that is consistent with its long and distinguished history.

SOCIAL DEMAND

AND HOW TO PROVIDE FOR IT

BRIAN ELLIS

PAMPHLETEER

© Brian Ellis 2016

Pamphleteer is an Australian Scholarly imprint.

First published 2016 by Australian Scholarly Publishing Pty Ltd
7 Lt Lothian St Nth, North Melbourne, Vic 3051
TEL: 03 9329 6963   FAX: 03 9329 5452
EMAIL: aspic@ozemail.com.au   WEB: scholarly.info

ISBN 978-1-925333-68-8

CONTENTS

INTRODUCTION

The social demand is what a government owes to its people. In any country that is governed by consent, it is contained in the government's social contract with its citizens. In a democracy, the citizens and the voting public are the same body of people, and the social demand just spells out what their entitlements are under this contract. If the society is one that is committed to upholding human rights, then the social demand must include everything that citizens are entitled to have, just in virtue of their humanity. And, a contract that creates such an entitlement is surely worth a great deal, provided that the government is in a position to deliver on its side of the bargain.

Social demand arises from the things that most people would want everyone in society to have. Really, it is a consequence of democracy itself that such demands should exist. In all democracies, governments seek election on the bases of certain *commitments, understandings,* and *promises* about what they will do. And, this involves *acceptance of past commitments,* which have not been specifically disavowed. There are also *established practices,* which everyone expects will continue, and there are *strong presumptions,* concerning what governments of all political persuasions will seek to do.

Until recently, it could have been assumed that all governments would seek to defend the nation's independence and way of life, try to promote the health and wellbeing of the nation in all of the sorts of ways it has been promoted in the past, aim to improve our knowledge, skills, and understanding, develop our culture and infrastructure, encourage people to participate fully in the workforce, develop people's potentialities, protect our natural environment, allow people to choose their ways of living without undue interference from others, seek to establish greater social equality, provide a first class infrastructure, and prevent animal cruelty. And, this list just scratches the surface. There are dozens of other things that governments are implicitly committed to doing. And, the sum total of all such current commitments constitutes what I am here calling the nation's *social contract*.

The social contract of a society is not a formal agreement. It is much more one-sided than that. Even so, in a robust democracy, such informal commitments can generally be relied upon to bind governments to their commitments, and thus establish a plausible concept of social demand, which can be used for planning purposes.

The extent of the social demand is the set of all goods and services that governments are implicitly obliged by their social contracts to secure. They do not, necessarily have to produce these social things themselves. In fact, most people would prefer to have sufficient resources to purchase their food, clothing and accommodation, rather than have it provided for them. The government's implicit commitment is just to ensure that everyone has enough resources to provide adequately for themselves for such items.

Until recently, every government felt obliged to ensure that there were adequate education, housing, and health care facilities in place, but with all the emphasis these days on self-reliance, on user pays, and on the apparent indifference of neoliberals to the fate of those who cannot find work they are capable of doing, homelessness has become a serious social problem. The social commitment to health care has fared much better. Our medicare system has so far proven to be adequate for the universal provision of such care. But recent governments have not shown the same respect for the nation's public education system. And, since neoliberalism has come to dominate social policy in Australia, the public system has been seriously downgraded. Consequently, there has been an exodus of middle-class children from state schools, and governments have greedily fed this trend by increasing their support for private school education at the expense of state schools. Government support for state schools has fallen well behind its support for private ones, and we now have, what is effectively a two-tier education system—a luxury one for the top 30% of income earners, and an impoverished, and greatly disadvantaged one for the children of the hoi polloi.

But social demand, as I understand it, is not only the demand for health, education and welfare services. It is the demand for all of the goods and services that governments are socially contracted to ensure should be adequately provided for. And, for any neoliberal society, the first of these has to be *employment opportunities*. For, without adequate employment for all able-bodied people, many people must languish in poverty, hopelessness, or forced to beg or prostitute themselves for the basic necessities of life. And when I speak of full employment, I do not mean what neoliberals and their economic spokespeople call 'full employment'. I mean *continuing full-time employment for everyone who needs to work full-time, and is fit and able to do it, and part-time employment to satisfy all other needs.* I am talking about full employment here in the sense in which we all enjoyed full employment, in the thirty years of the welfare state era, from 1945 to 1975, when unemployment averaged just 2.0%.

PART I

SOCIAL DEMAND

Social goods and services are things that governments are committed by their social contracts to providing. Some of these things are provided by volunteer agencies, and some are inevitably provided by the relatives of people in need. Naturally, governments welcome support of charities and family members, because it reduces the amount they would otherwise have to raise in taxes and charges to pay for it.

But such relief services do not paint the right picture. For, nearly all of the money spent on providing social goods and services in response to social demand is used to fund government institutions, agencies, and programs, many of which are long-established, and were set up many years ago to develop the country as a viable and cohesive society. Police forces and prison systems, for example, must be supported to maintain law and order. A military establishment is needed to secure the realm, deal with threats to stability in our region, and to deter any would-be aggressors.[1] An educational system is needed that will allow students to develop their knowledge, understanding, and practical skills to the limits of their natural capacities, and to provide them with the training they will need to flourish as individuals in a modern democratic society—whatever their talents may be, and whatever their cultural backgrounds. As well as all of these things, a good society needs a first-rate health care system that will deliver good health services cheaply and affordably to everyone. It also needs a well-developed infrastructure for the delivery of essential services, such as water, electricity, gas, the internet, transport (road, rail, sea, and air). And these are, all of them, social goods and services, whose maintenance and development are needed for the health of the nation.

The level of social supply required for all of this social demand, which governments of all political stripes are (or used to be) committed to providing, is evidently huge. And, it goes well beyond the range of social goods and services that I have listed here. It must, for example, also include fire brigades, country fire authorities, ambulance services, paramedical services, drug abuse and rehabilitation facilities, research establishments, women's refuges, and so on, and on, and on.

It is obvious, therefore, that the business model of government is inapt. Neoliberalism is a system of government that recognizes no demand other than economic demand. For their view is that no social goods or services are legitimate claims on the government (or governments) of the nation, beyond the defence of the realm, the maintenance of law and order, unless there is a sufficient economic demand for them. And, this was always a very radical thesis. It was, I believe, an extreme reaction to the even more radical socialist agendas in the USSR, Mainland China, and Indochina. And, it threatens the ability of Western nations to respond adequately to the social demands they are socially contractually required now to supply.

In any society in which economic demand is the dominant force, social demand must inevitably be neglected. And we, in Australia, are in a bind, because the business model of government is not primarily interested in providing adequately for the wellbeing of all of the nation's citizens. It does not see itself as being in loco parentis in the nation, with unconditional love for its children, and determined to do the best it can for them. It sees itself, rather, as the board of management of a corporation in charge of a multinational business, with a workforce led by union heavies out to extract as much as they can from the nation's economy for their members' selfish interests. And its primary task, they think, once the basics have been taken care of, is to make the nation competitive with others on the world stage, so that it can make a substantial return to its shareholders, i.e. its taxpayers. As Tony Abbott once said, 'Australia is open for business.'

Social Demand is supposed to be a measure of what people really need for themselves, for their dependents, and for the society in which they live, for them to live proudly in their society with freedom and dignity. So, there must inevitably be reference to a somewhat vague notion of 'community standards' in any attempt to define social demand. There is some hope, however, that we may be able to agree about *minimal* standards. For no one with a social conscience would want to live in a society in which people languished in poverty, disease or hunger. Most people would much rather live in a flourishing society, in which everyone was able to live as well as their natural talents would allow. But this is probably too ambitious. So, let us focus upon minimal standards of living and wellbeing. For such standards have at least some chance of becoming generally recognized, and therefore of being government guaranteed.

It is true that many of the sorts of things we all need basically are things we can buy, if we have the money to do so. And, moreover, we would not want it any other way, because the commercially available goods we need are mostly things we should want to choose for ourselves. But, to purchase the commercial goods or services we need, we all must have sufficiently good and reliable sources of income, such as a well-paid job with tenure, a pension, or a guaranteed income under some sort of guaranteed minimum income scheme. So, the right to a steady and continuing income is, perhaps, one of the primary social goods that any modern society could possibly provide.

Indeed, it is an implied human right of people living in social democracies like our own. Article 22 of the Universal Declaration of Human Rights (UDHR) says that

> Everyone, as a member of society, has the right to social security, and is entitled to realization, through national effort and international cooperation, and in accordance with the resources of each state, of the economic, social and cultural rights indispensable for his[/her] dignity and the free development of his[/her] personality.

But it is impossible to live with dignity, or be free to develop one's own personality in a social democracy, if one does not have adequate means.

Social goods and services are not to be confused with the economic ones, which can be measured with some precision by statisticians. The GDP for any given country, for example, is simply the sum total of all goods and services produced in that country for the year in question. The measure of the yearly economic demand for locally produced goods and services arising within a country is therefore given by the country's GDP minus the value of its exports for that year. And this is a nice exact figure. But current social demand is very different. Its estimation requires projection. It requires, for example, an estimate of how much additional expenditure on employment creation, or on subsidies, etc. would be needed to provide a program intended to ensure that everyone would be able to live as well as their natural talents would reasonably allow (given our present circumstances), what percentage of this expenditure could reasonably (in the circumstances) be expected to be regained eventually by increased taxes on increased earnings, and what more would really be needed (in our present circumstances) to create a society we could mostly feel proud of.

1.1. The Architecture of Goods and Services

In her book *The Six Capitals* (2014), Jane Gleeson-White has proposed a six-category classification of social and economic goods. Her aim was to account adequately for the production of all of the goods and services in an economy, including all of the costs and benefits (direct or indirect) of all of the productive activities taking place in any modern society. She chose to do this by generalising the concept of capital, so that a score sheet, which includes capital gains and losses in each of these categories could, in principle, be drawn up in a comprehensive accountancy report. Gleeson-White listed six different capitals: natural, financial, manufactured, intellectual, human, and social/relationship capital.

However, I do not think that her conceptual scheme provides

a good framework for an integrated outlook of the kind she seeks. For production in a capitalist country is always in response to demand, and the best way of categorising the different kinds of goods and services is by means of the different kinds of demand it supplies. Economic demand defines the realm of commercial goods and services. Social contractual demand effectively defines the realm of social goods and services.

I would have no objection to including natural capital as a separate category, if we were drawing up a list of things that are good for business. For clearly some natural phenomena, and even some innate human characteristics (such as beauty or persuasiveness), may be good for business. But natural phenomena do not qualify as goods or services, because they are not products of human endeavour. A beautiful landscape is an advantage to the tourist industry. But it is not a product, and so not anything that could be counted as 'a good' or 'a kind of service' in the sense in which these terms are used in economic theory. It is a good only in the sense of being *a good thing*. But lots of things are good (evaluatively), which are not goods in the sense of products. Many economic goods are in fact not good at all—atom bombs, for example. And, this is true also of many social goods and services. Some just fail lamentably to achieve the social purposes for which they were created

The word 'capital', just like the word 'good', is ambiguous. It is sometimes used as an evaluative term, and sometimes as a technical one. For 'capital' sometimes means having market value, where it is not evaluative, and sometimes being accumulatively more valuable, where it is evaluative. It seems to me that Gleeson-White's list must have been drawn up using the evaluative sense. But, if one focuses on the accumulative sense, then, in drawing up a list of capitals, one might be asking: In what ways can a society become cumulatively richer and more prosperous? And then it would be easy to arrive at Gleeson-White's list, (if this were the methodology she used). For, of each of her categories, it would be entirely appropriate to say of many countries we admire that they are rich in one or more of her capitals. Her categories are 'natural capital', 'financial capital', 'manufactured capital', 'intellectual capital' and 'social/relationship capital'. And, it is easy to think of countries that are rich in some or all of these ways

But if we wish to employ concepts of goods and services that are formally just like those of manufactured or financial goods, then we need to identify the kind of demand that leads to their creation. In a neoliberal society, all manufactured and financial goods are created in response to economic demand. The only other category of demand that generates goods and services would appear to be that of social demand, which originates from the social contract of the nation. For social goods must be understood as referring to all enduring social products, and these social products must be understood as being, for example, the institutions, agencies and programs created to produce the social services that are required to satisfy social demand—whether that demand be good or bad, justified or unjustified. And such social goods, and the services they produce, are clearly to be distinguished from all commercial goods and services, not by their use or usefulness, but by the nature of the demand they were created to supply.

The social goods, thus understood, are essentially different from the commercial ones. Yet overall they are strikingly similar. For there is a pattern involving rights to goods and services—commercial rights in the case of commercial goods and services, and social contractual rights in the case of social goods and services. In the commercial realm, the purchaser of goods or services acquires (in the act of buying them) the right to be supplied with the purchased goods. This right derives from a commercial contract. In the social realm, there exists a kind of social contract between the people and their government. And, as I have argued, such a social contract must exist in any society in which human rights are respected. For, in every such society, the government has a prima facie moral obligation to uphold, and provide for, the human rights that are accepted. And, the people do not need to do or buy anything to acquire their human rights. They have them as a matter of right. And, the government must be willing: (a) to ensure that the social needs of the community are adequately supplied, and (b) to guarantee that everyone has an on-going source of income adequate to supply themselves and their dependents with at least their regular daily needs.

Both kinds of things can be said to have value. If there are two kinds of goods, then there are also two kinds of values, commercial and social values. Moreover, for each of these kinds of values, there are distinctive kinds of contractual goods. The distinctive goods of the broad social category are those of social contractual rights, e.g. human rights and land rights, and the institutions (hospitals, clinics, universities, research institutes etc.), and the rest, that are created to supply them.

Finally, the social goods, like the commercial ones, exist in two primary forms: as contractual goods, and as realised goods.

The commercial contractual goods are stocks, shares, mortgages, and so on, which themselves can be bought or sold. These are the sorts of things that Gleeson-White calls 'financial capital'. But there is no equivalent of financial capital in the social realm. For, social goods or services cannot be bought or sold, in the sort of way that stocks, shares and mortgages can be.

A sound economic theory should, I think, have places within it for all of these different kinds of goods and services, and for the full range of providers of such goods and services. For, assuredly, they all exist, and perform important commercial or social functions in every modern society. That is, a decent theory has to deal with the contributions of stock exchanges, solicitors, titles offices and banks to commercial practices. But it also requires both individual and collective providers of social services. Individual providers of social services may be either paid or volunteer, and collective social service providers must include governments at various levels, and specialist institutions (either paid or voluntary) for the delivery of social services. The specialist institutions required include the universities, hospitals, medical clinics, pharmacists, law courts, armies, police forces, schools, research establishments, and so on.

Governments clearly have distinctive roles in the economy of a country. For our governments are the owners of all of the land that is occupied by the nation, and, between them, federal, state and local governments are ultimately responsible for ensuring that all of the nation's professionals, corporations and institutions perform their allotted functions well and efficiently. It should be noted, however, that when a government claims that it is releasing land for sale, it speaks misleadingly. For no land can be sold to a citizen of the nation in which this land is situated. A land right, or title to land, may be sold. But no government can allow its individual or corporate citizens to literally own the land, without establishing rights that conflict with their own. The land could, in principle, be sold to a foreign country, which is what happened in the case of Alaska, when its sovereignty was transferred from Russia to the USA.

Plots of land (but not their boundaries) are essentially parts of nature, and to purchase a plot of land is essentially just to obtain a certificate of title, which permits the so-called 'land-owner' to fence it off and occupy it, to apply for planning or building permits, or to plant crops, if it is agricultural land, or to graze livestock, if it is farmland. But the land still remains, essentially the property of the state, and it could, at any time, reclaim that land, if there were good reasons for doing so—or even if there were none.

Yet, according to all standard economic models, governments are not even players in the economic system. They are said to be exogenous, and their contributions to the economy of the nation is classified as an externality. This is surely a monstrous distortion of reality. Economic theorists must eventually develop more realistic theories, however much they go against the established grain. Governments are primarily responsible for supplying the social demands of the nation, and this fact should be acknowledged in every macroeconomic model.

1.2. Social Goods and Services

The simplest, and most fundamental kind of contract is a one-sided affair. And, the primitive social contracts of governments are fundamental in this way. Their standing commitments are to their people—in respect of their social, civil, political, economic, and cultural rights, privileges, freedoms, and so on. On the other hand, citizens have their roles too. The standing commitments of citizens to the states in which they live are their loyalties to the state, and their willingness to promote it (e.g. by paying taxes or defending its interests, especially in times of crisis). For a stable society, these levels of commitment must be accepted as complementary, so that each is thought to be sufficient to support the other. Any free trade deal that allows international corporations to exploit Australia's social contract, but to avoid contributing to its maintenance and development, must therefore be grossly unjust, and therefore destabilizing.

The primary social contractual goods in any society are human rights (e.g. those listed in the *Universal Declaration*), and land rights. These goods, like banknotes, are all contractual in nature, although we do not carry credit cards to acknowledge them. And a nation that honors its human rights obligations by supplying the Australian people with the kinds of goods and services these rights entail must inevitably be richer socially. It is possible for a nation to be rich commercially, but poor socially, or conversely. Saudi Arabia and other Arab countries in Middle East are cases in point. Australia is rich commercially, but it is rapidly becoming much poorer socially, as a consequence of its treatment of asylum seekers, and its failure to provide adequate income support for all. China and India are, I believe, rapidly improving their positions, both commercially and socially. But the stand-out examples of countries that are rich both commercially and socially are the Scandinavian ones, and Japan.

It is also possible for the human rights of some people to be taken away from them by others, as happened frequently in colonial days, and has happened more recently (a) in the occupied territories in the former state of Palestine, and (b) the citizens of Syria and Iraq who have been terrorized by a marauding group of thugs, who have no respect for even the most basic of human rights.

Our social rights are never commercial. *They are essentially ongoing in a way that commercial rights cannot be.* A government's social indebtedness to its citizens can never be paid in full, because social rights are ongoing, whereas commercial rights are never essentially so. If I owe you money, then you have a commercial right to receive it. And, in principle, I can pay my debt in full. And then, of course, I no longer owe you anything. But if citizens have claims against the government in virtue of their human rights, or land rights, then no amount of government action can ever banish these claims. Human rights continue to exist for people for as long as they live. So their rights must continue to exist, even if for the time being they are satisfied. Indeed, this is the important difference between a human right and a commercial one. A commercial right can be fulfilled, but a human right can only be satisfied for the time being. I am not saying that human rights are infinite entitlements. They are simply different in nature from commercial rights. They are essentially ongoing.

Nevertheless, there is some similarity between human rights and on-going commercial contracts. Thus, if an insurance company sells me a retirement pension of $400 per week for the rest of my life, then I acquire an ongoing commercial right. But my human rights are not like this. Retirement pensions have an ongoing character, that is true. But human rights are necessarily rights we think everyone should have, and be the same for everyone, and not things for which anyone in particular must pay. So human rights are different from retirement pensions. They are universal, owed by governments, free of direct costs to individuals, and non-negotiable.

Nevertheless, the bill for maintaining the required machinery for human rights maintenance might well be largely met by a national insurance scheme that guaranteed everyone a certain minimum wage for the whole of their adult lives. To achieve this, one would need only an income tax regime that increased people's incomes to, say, $400 per week, if they should fall below that figure (negative taxation), but was otherwise progressive, beginning to become subject to normal income tax at, say, $700 per week, thus providing those subsisting on $400 per week with strong incentive to become more gainfully employed. Such schemes have been suggested before, and might go some considerable way towards providing for the basic social demand that exists in every modern society.

Nevertheless, any attempt to dispense with human rights, and replace them with a guaranteed minimum income scheme, would be wrong. For human rights provide for much more than just adequate money to live on. Governments are, or should be, committed to giving everyone a real chance of realizing their full potential, as well as living freely, and with dignity, in their own societies.

This discussion of social rights inevitably leads us on to consider our rights to employment. The issues are complex, and I will discuss them in Part II of this paper. In my view, full employment can be achieved, even in a society that is not growing very much (if at all). What is needed, I will argue, is a strategy that requires governments to engage in programs that are specifically designed to: (a) employ those who are currently unemployed in the towns and suburbs where most of them live; (b) provide them with real opportunities to do some much needed work; and (c) present them with work choices that are realistically suited to their education, fitness and abilities. One suggestion is that the Federal Government should institute a national program to keep old people, everywhere in their own homes for as long as possible.

But this is just one suggestion. And, it is not difficult to think of things that need doing in our society, which would provide good and sustainable work for people with skills of the kinds that most people already have, or could easily acquire. It is just that such work is not very fashionable today. It is not high tech, and it mainly involves maintaining or fixing things, or otherwise doing things that young people have not yet learnt to do, old people are no longer able to do, busy people do not have time to do, pregnant people would find it hard to do, and injured people will not be able to do, until they recover. The Federal Government might, for example, sponsor a program, to upgrade the quality and state of repair of all of the pubic buildings in all of the poorer towns and suburbs of the nation, and to improve the recreation facilities available to all of the residents. For clearly such work exists wherever people live in numbers, and most people, would normally be able to take some pride in doing it.

In countries governed by consent, there are at least five broad classes of institutions involved in the delivery of social services:

(a) the governments themselves, (b) the institutions of defence and law enforcement, (c) those of law and its administration, (d) the institutions of health and health delivery, and (e) educational institutions. Let us review them briefly:

(a) *The governments themselves.* In social democracies the governments represent the people, and one of their primary concerns must be to administer these institutions in the public interest.

(b) *The nation's armed forces.* There is a complex group of armed forces in every modern society. They all have their own specialist social functions, and it is their job to deliver these services as well and efficiently as possible.

(c) The overall system of civilian protection also includes *the legal system.* The legal system consists of the law courts, law schools, prisons, and detention centres. So, their work must also be considered to be productive (whether or not you approve of them). In my view, detention centres are socially disastrous. But social production is no less likely to be of things we don't want than commercial production.

(d) *The health care institutions.* These include all of the nation's hospitals, hospices, respite care facilities, nursing homes, as well as the medical staff and distaff training schools they require. And all are, of course, involved, directly or indirectly in the production of social services.

(e) *The educational institutions.* Many of them, at primary and secondary level are privately owned. But governments are ultimately responsible for all of the schools, universities, research institutes, teacher training facilities, kindergartens, and technical colleges of the nation.

Every country has literally hundreds of such institutions, and their maintenance and development are necessary parts of the social welfare program of every modern society.

But the government's responsibilities for the delivery of social services do not end with their commitments to security, law and order, health care, and education. All of the infrastructure that is built by, or for, governments is delivering social services. The building of infrastructure is not normally thought of as involving the delivery of social services. But, in practice, most built infrastructure has been made available to the general public, and most of it has been paid for by governments at some level—state, federal or local. But infrastructure projects often produce goods that could equally well be commercial ones. Their purpose is to provide social services to the people who use them. So, most of our infrastructure must be considered to be made up of social goods too. For social services do not have to be services that are directed only to socially dependent people. Much of it is actually a service to the able-bodied and socially competent.

In this age of neoliberalism, we have been taught to think of social services as providing for the poor, the young, the weak, the old, or the disabled. But that is wrong. With rare exceptions, the schools, universities, hospitals, etc. and the roads, railway tracks, reservoirs, water pipes, sewerage works, kiosks, walking tracks, ski-trails, outlooks, and resting places are all public facilities, and nearly all of them were constructed by governments for the benefit of the general public. They are no less social than the wheelchair ramps and playgrounds, which fit more naturally into the neoliberal picture.

1.3. Social Contractual Goods

Human and animal rights are all contractual too, but not contractual in the way that commercial agreements are. If a society is committed to upholding human rights, then these commitments must become included in the society's social contract. Such contracts are almost never written down. For, governments like to leave themselves free to act in radically new ways, if the occasion should ever demand it. In any case, the task of specifying what precisely is to be expected of governments to fulfill their obligations would be huge, and perhaps unproductive. But the difficulty of tabulating what is to be expected of governments does not mean that it does not have any prior commitments. Normally, they have a great many. For, the governments of all societies that are ruled by consent are expected to act according to the expectations of their citizens, unless they have specific mandates to do otherwise. Therefore, without doing anything at all, new governments inherit commitments from their predecessors. They inherit the laws that have been enacted by them, the institutions they have set up to serve the people, the commitments they have made to their electorates, the treaties they have signed, and so on. Thus, in every society that is ruled by consent there exists a kind of understanding concerning the responsibilities of governments.

This understanding is what I call the social contract of a society. And, the social contractual goods produced to supply social demands included in this social contract are important contributors to the wellbeing of everyone.

In general, the social goods in a community are among the things that the members of that community need, if they are to live good and satisfying lives. Some of these things, such as food or shelter, are *material goods*, which can be bought or sold. So, if people have a readily available source of income, there may be no need to legislate for their provision. But many are not material, and cannot be traded. Some good things, such as health, beauty, education, intelligence, ability to speak the local language, are *natural or acquired characteristics*. One can pay to protect one's health, acquire a better education, or learn a language. But these things can be possessed only as characteristics, never as things that can be traded. If one lacks any of the natural goods, such as good looks, eloquence in the language, or whatever, then one may seek to acquire them, but failing that, one is naturally at a disadvantage. The social goods also include a number of *positional goods*—those attaching to one's role or position in life—viz. the rights, powers, freedoms, privileges, guarantees and opportunities one has in virtue of one's social position. For these may or may not exist in any given community, and may be more or less well provided for, if they do. But they are not in general things that have a price, even though they may cost money to administer or exercise.

Normally, our demands for social services have to be determined by how much we need them to flourish as individuals. But the quantity of this need is not measurable in any straightforward way. So, it is not an economic variable. Nevertheless, its determination is what democracy is all about; and most democratic governments have evolved strategies for determining the social needs and priorities of their members in their various electorates.

To evaluate social needs, our representatives must exercise their social consciences, and think about how people normally relate to one another, depending on their circumstances. First and foremost, they need money, and a regular source of income, so that they are not left wanting for any of the basics of life—food, shelter, clothing, means of transport, insurance, and so on. They also need money to correct or compensate for any lack of natural or acquired social goods, so that they can interact with others in normal ways. But sometimes money is not enough. People with disabilities need disabled stickers for their cars, disabled access to buildings, and so on. And these, of course, are positional goods, all designed to improve the lives of people who are disadvantaged in this sort of way. Pregnant women, children with learning difficulties, refugees from other lands, and dozens of other groups in every society also need special facilities. And these are all positional social goods.

Of special interest are the social goods that every member of society has a right to. If we are fortunate enough to live in a society in which all human rights are guaranteed, or adequately provided for, then we have come a long way towards achieving our goal of providing for the full spectrum of the social goods needed for any good society. Our civil and political rights guarantee our basic freedoms, the democratic structure of our politics, and the fairness of our legal system. And our economic, social and cultural rights guarantee the basic adequacy and fairness of our social institutions, including our schools, universities, health care system, and ways of treating minorities.

1.4. Social Rights and Obligations

In the aftermath of World War II, the Great Depression, and the ghastly revelations of the Holocaust, the United Nations was formed, and set about building a framework for peace and security in the world which would pay due respect to the dignity of humankind. There were to be no more holocausts. The key to peace and security, they believed, was to try earnestly to discover what the nations of the world really believed about how societies should be structured, and to articulate the powers and responsibilities that they thought their governments should have ideally vis-à-vis their people. The resulting document containing their findings became the *Universal Declaration of Human Rights*, and was adopted by the General Assembly of the United Nations without dissent in December 1948.

There was never a clear agreement in the UN about what human rights really are. But the representatives of the governments on the drafting committee chaired by Eleanor Roosevelt were encouraged not to concern themselves too much with the philosophy of human rights, and to proceed intuitively to formulate the principles that they thought should actually apply. There could therefore be a question about what they had really achieved. But, whatever the status of the human rights they finally arrived at, it was commonly thought that the resolution they agreed upon was a huge step toward defining the responsibilities of governments to the people they governed (citizens, residents, visitors, refugees, etc.), and setting reasonable limits upon their authority over them.

The thought behind this document was that a decent world, fit for human beings, would require most states to have social structures in which people could flourish, and live with dignity according to their own traditions. There were 48 votes in favour of the convention, eight abstentions, and two non-voters. The abstainers were six of the world's then communist states,[2] as well as Saudi Arabia and the Union of South Africa. The abstentions of the six communist states, led by the Soviet Union, reflected their common view that the document did not go far enough. They wanted it to outlaw fascism, which it did not, and so did not condemn the militaristic regimes they had fought so hard, and with such great sacrifice, to defeat. This was understandable, and personally I am inclined to agree with them on this point. But I fully accept the pragmatic approach to the development of the doctrine of human rights taken by the UN, and, like Dr Evatt, I believe that it is better to have a widely accepted convention on human rights to work with than no convention at all.

James Allen has argued, quite rightly, that all human rights are soft and fluffy statements with which almost anyone could agree. Therefore, their acceptance is compatible with almost any kind of state that anyone might prefer. Of course they are, given its method of construction. But, in his review of my book on *Social Humanism*, Tony Lynch (2012/13, pp. 28-31) turns this nicely to my advantage. Here, reproduced with Lynch's approval, is what he says:

> If neo-liberalism is on the rack empirically—we are not all getting better off—and if accepting its story undermines that generalised benevolence in which it is packaged, then unless we want to live in a world of empty words and naked power we need a new moral story; one which implies a genuine, rather than specious, community of interests. We do not need to start from scratch, for we have, if fading, some memory of social democracy; and its remnant institutions surround us, if dilapidated and under attack. We need a coherent, persuasive, moral story which—unlike in the past— isn't a jerry-rigged pragmatic middle way compromise

between socialism and laissez-faire, but has a depth, an integrity and completeness, of the kind neo-liberalism purported to have and, for 30 years, and convinced many it did have.

It is this story Tony Judt calls for in *Ill Fares the Land*, and it is what Brian Ellis aims to provide in *Social Humanism*.

This isn't the place for an extended analysis and commentary on what—necessarily, given Ellis' ambitions—is a complex and deeply argued text.

I leave that for the scholarly journals. I want instead to situate Ellis' story against the earlier efforts of John Rawls and Jurgen Habermas to provide social democracy with the moral story it needs.

Let us begin with John Rawls and A Theory of Justice (1971).[3] Rawls invites us to perform a thought-experiment. He asks us to imagine ourselves behind a veil of ignorance, which removes from us all personal knowledge. While we know we are someone behind the veil, we do not know which someone we are, nor our place in social life, and so cannot be biased towards ourselves in terms of personal preferences or social and economic position. Behind the veil we are in the Original Position. This is the position in which, all being unbiased, any unanimous agreement we make is such that once the veil is lifted we are bound to accept it as fair and just.

Rawls argues that what would emerge from behind the veil would be a state—a social democratic state, though Rawls, being an American, doesn't use the term—characterized by two principles of justice.

The first principle is the Principle of Equal Liberty: we would all agree (and so it is fair and just) to the most amount of individual liberty compatible with a like liberty for all. This seems reasonable: not knowing who I am or what I want or where I will be in society after the veil is removed, I will want as much freedom as possible to be the kind of person I will find myself to be. And, as I could be anyone, I will want everyone to have this freedom. This principle doesn't give us anything especially social-democratic. It is perfectly compatible with neo-liberalism. It can even be argued that it is neo-liberalism.[4]

But a second principle, Rawls argues, emerges from the Original Position, and it is this principle which makes his account of justice a social democratic one. Here is that principle:

Social and economic inequalities are to be arranged so that (a) they are to be of the greatest benefit of the least-advantaged members of society (the difference principle), (b) offices and positions must be open to everyone under conditions of fair equality of opportunity. Rawls assumes that if we value individual freedom, we must allow that freedom will produce various kinds of inequalities not only because choices may go well or ill but because often we will be interested in making very different choices.

The question is how, behind the veil, we would think about this; and the second principle of justice provides the answer. Socially we would insist on genuine equality of opportunity, and economically we would insist that inequality is only fair for all, even those with little, if those very inequalities make even those with very little better off than they would be with some more equal distribution of income and wealth. This is boilerplate social democracy, and it might seem we have the moral story social democracy needs, and so Ellis is reinventing the wheel.

But he isn't. He isn't, because Rawls story leaves us helpless, defenceless, against those real political and economic forces social democracy seeks to tame, and neo-liberalism exploits.

The 2nd principle—the Difference Principle in particular—has no moral and political bite. The Difference

Principle says inequalities in income and wealth are not merely OK, but positively desirable, so long as those inequalities make the worst-off better off than they would be under some other, more equal, set of economic arrangements. And here is the problem: for in any system of serious inequalities those who have the most will certainly insist (they will have founded think tanks, hired economists and other public relations flacks, to "prove" this) that their riches make the poorest around here (you know, the hungry, homeless, sick and uninsured) better off than they would be if things were different.

Can't the poor object? Of course they can![5] But who will they hire to fight back? How can they show that they would be better off under some other, less unequal, system when they have to admit that their proposed system—not being the actual system—is merely an imagined possibility? In this game the rich always win. Not only is Rawls› moral story no threat to them, they can appeal to it to justify their riches and everyone else›s poverty.

The lesson for social democracy is that thought experiments, acts of imagination, are at best, tractionless in the face of real economic and political forces, at worse acts of collusion. The lesson—Ellis takes it to heart—is that social democracy must be situated in that world in which it fights for its existence and strives for success. The moral story of social democracy is a real, not an imagined, story, and it is the story of real, not imaginary, people. As Ellis says:

the social moral principles we now accept depend mainly on what social decisions were actually made in the past, what we now feel comfortable with, and what we would like to be preserved in future. That is, morality must be seen as an evolving system—evolving as societies shift their policies to adapt to environmental or social change."[6]

Placing the moral story of social democracy in history and practice is not only the right way to go, it is the only way.

It's not that there is nothing in Rawls that is useful. There is, and Ellis exploits this. For while Rawls sets things in Never-Never Land, he is surely right to think of morality in terms of ideals (of the kind of person we want to be, and the kind of world we want to live in with others), and to think of these ideals as the core of that deep social contract on which all genuine community arises and depends.

In Ellis' hands this social contract lies at the heart of social democracy. "Every society" he says, "that is governed by consent has a real social contract of some kind". "Think of this contract as a complete true anthropological description of the society, what its institutions are, what people's understandings are of their rights, obligations, and responsibilities, what its values, laws, and customs are, and everything else that is relevant to understanding how the society works…"

Now from the point of view of the people who live in that society, rather than the anthropologist, "the best society will be the one with the best social contract. It is reasonable, therefore, for the members of any society to seek to improve their society's social contract."[7]

This is exactly right.

Naturally, I agree with all of this. And, in my view, the *UDHR* should be regarded always as a work in progress, not as a legal document, but as a guide to where we are in the ongoing process in developing strategies for human advancement. In this respect, it is an invaluable guide, and Allan does a great disservice to the cause of social democratic evolution to rubbish it. Of course it sounds 'soft and fluffy', or 'wet' if you are Margaret Thatcher, or 'hopelessly idealistic' if you are a tough-minded businessman or woman. But this does not mean that it should be ignored. If it is soft and fluffy, then it strikes exactly the right chord. It is so, because it sounds *good*, and *fair*, and *highly desirable*. But what else could you possibly expect in a document, such as the *UDHR*, intended to define a moral position.

It turned out that the only strong ideological opposition to any of the Articles of the *UDHR* came from South Africa, which thought that the declaration was manifestly incompatible with its Apartheid regime, and Saudi Arabia, because it would have allowed Muslims to convert to other religions, or renounce their religion altogether (which were then capital offences). But even these states did not vote against the final resolution. They were not then, and probably never will be, the only states that the world thinks are out of line. Most of the world thinks that the US and the UK are out of line on a whole lot of issues, although in some ways much better than most. But it is important that we should keep our ideals in mind, if we don't want to go in any of the ways that the naked powerbrokers of the world want to take us. The *UDHR* is a vision for a peaceful and prosperous world, not a document for the High Courts of nation states to use to determine the validity of legislation. But if we were actually to design such a document, surely the *UDHR* would be the natural starting point. And, so it should be for almost every country.

As I understand them, human rights are informal agreements, which we should like to see incorporated in the social contracts of all nations. So, the methodology adopted by the drafting committee was entirely appropriate. They are manifestly not actual agreements between governments and the people for whom they are responsible. But there are such things as social laws and conventions (which may or may not be written down), which, nevertheless, may have something of the force of agreements. Mostly, they are demanded by the force of public opinion, rather than by the laws of the land. But obedience to these laws or conventions could be enforced by international law, if the members of any society so wished. Few governments, however, are willing to bind themselves in this way, since the human rights of individuals, so enacted into law, would naturally translate into the moral duties of governments to the individuals who have these rights (Ellis, 2012). Canada did, in fact, enact the *UDHR*, but Australia did not.

The full realization of any human right would obviously be an important social achievement, and therefore a social good. But social goods such as these are not at all like commercial goods. Commercial goods are enduring particulars that can be bought or sold. But provisions for human rights cannot be bought or sold—although they may be more or less expensive to provide for, or enforce. The human rights that may need enforcing are the so-called negative rights of the *UDHR*. These rights define our various freedoms: e.g. freedom of thought and expression, freedom of association, and so on. The positive rights, such as those of education and health care, are the rights that governments are committed to providing as adequately as they can for the people they serve. But I am not sure that this distinction is very useful. Better is the distinction between political and civil rights, on the one hand, and economic, social and cultural rights, on the other. And, the *UDHR* is structured with this distinction in mind. There are, in fact thirty articles in the charter, beginning with the civil and political rights, and concluding with social, economic, and cultural rights of humankind.

The rights now accorded to animals are clearly not as extensive as those set out for humans in the *UDHR*, because animals generally lack human understanding, and, in various ways, human sensitivities. They are not completely without these attributes, however. So, we willingly extend some basically human rights to other species for the same reason that we extend them to the members of other societies. We empathize with many animals, and appreciate the sources of their distress, even though we may not fully comprehend it. As David Hume once observed, empathy is a powerful motivator of social choice.

Cruel and inhumane treatment is abhorrent to us, and always has been. And it is no less abhorrent when it is meted out to animals, even to those that are not our pets. The grossly indecent treatment of alleged sinners in medieval times was generally regarded as abhorrent, even back then, as is evident by the depictions of hell in medieval works of art. Let us not create a hell on Earth for animals.

1.5. Human Goods

Human capital is a kind of social good. It refers to the size and developed characteristics of the human community that is being considered. To describe a human community properly for the purpose of gauging its productive capacity, it would be necessary to create a comprehensive social profile of its population vis-à-vis its business, manufacturing and trading activities, as they currently stand. Profiles would be needed concerning the quality and potential size of the workforce, the skills it has, its educational and intellectual achievements, its moral character (e.g. its honesty, trustworthiness, reliability, and so on), its motivation to succeed, willingness to work, conscientiousness, and so on. Fairly clearly, a society that scores well in the human capital dimension will be more productive than one that scores badly.

But a full report on the human capital of a given society need not be limited to these obviously work-related attitudes, skills, or capacities. It might also contain some information about people's attitudes to one another—their degrees of tolerance of religious, social, ethnic, or cultural differences, for example. Or, it might be relevant to know what the gender breakdown of the population is, how this affects the gender breakdown of the workforce, and how willing or able people of different gender or sexuality are to work together.

I appreciate that these aspects of a human capital report might well be given separately—for example, under the heading of 'Social Relations Goods', which, I think, is roughly what Gleeson-White had in mind. But it does not matter here whether this is true or not, provided that social goods of such a moral nature are properly taken into account in the overall social profile of the society. To achieve this result, my inclination is to develop a separate category of goods relating specifically to the moral virtues. For, these have been widely discussed in the philosophical literature, and there is no doubting their centrality to moral philosophy. I envisioned that this category would deal with the extent to which our common moral precepts are socially acted upon in the community.

It is reasonable to suppose that the quality of the human capital in a society is a product of its educational system. So, it is entirely appropriate that we should think of human capital as a social good—one that can and should be produced and nurtured in any given society. If it is developed, then it may not only contribute to the productivity of the workforce, but also to increasing the quality and of the work they do, and the satisfaction they obtain in doing it.

1.6. The Goods of Morality

The social virtues (such as compassion, beneficence, kindliness, helpfulness, truthfulness, honesty, trust, and so on) all contribute to the wellbeing of citizens, and hence to the good of society. In my view, these social virtues are all purely social, and the driving force behind them is our desire for social goods. However, it has not been fashionable to think, as I do, of the virtues as social goods. Normally, the virtues are supposed to be characteristics of individuals, and so good for them, as individuals. So, many people would think of them as good *personal attributes*, i.e. as attributes that make individuals better people, rather than as social products that make societies better for everyone.

But, as I see it, good moral behaviour is good because it is creative of social goods—goods that derive most of their value from the contributions they make to community living, which are worth cultivating for their positive utility. Interestingly, the opposites of these traits are all social vices, which detract from the benefits that flow from the actions of those driven by the socially virtuous. We all, therefore, have a social interest in promoting the social virtues of individuals, and discouraging the development of social vices.

I am not denying that there are personal virtues and vices. For, there are such things as self-improvement and self-harm.

Naturally, I think that a tendency to the first is a virtue, while a tendency to the second is a vice. But these are not, necessarily, *social* virtues or vices. In some cases, they really are *personal* ones. For what is essentially good about self-improvement is that it makes people better and happier in themselves, not that it adds to the wellbeing of people generally. And, conversely, what is essentially bad about self-harm is that it harms the harmer, and it would do that, whether or not there were a society to be affected by it.

The idea that our basic values are social rather than personal is one that I have been arguing now for some years. Simply put, the position for which I argued in *Social Humanism* (2012) is that our moral precepts are essentially just principles of socially acceptable behaviour that we should wish to see entrenched in the social contracts of all nations. This is, of course, not an objectivist metaphysical claim. But its subjectivism is not defeatist. On the contrary, I argued that it is more realistic about the diversity of moral stances, and the historical causes of such disagreements. It explains the facts of moral evolution, offers hope of achieving a global consensus on a core set of moral issues, and a vision that it may, one day, be possible to reach agreement on a globally valid social contract, that would be acceptable to all nations. The *UDHR*, I thought, is a precursor of the Social Structure section of such a contract.

1.7. Social Relationships

Good social relationships are also of great importance for human wellbeing. For the values of love, friendship, companionship, understanding, and empathy are all worth cultivating for the social good they create. A society in which such networks of social relationships are able to develop and flourish is always better than one in which barriers of various kinds lead to social exclusion. A good society, therefore, must be an *inclusive* one. To create an inclusive society, I argued (Ellis, 2012), it is necessary to remove all class distinctions and the kinds of inequality that would effectively deny the normal kinds of reciprocation that characterize good social relationships.

A good society, I also argued, must be one that is strongly egalitarian. It must, I said, provide for what I called 'real equality of opportunity'. Weak equality of opportunity exists in a society in which everyone is *equal in and before the law*. A stronger conception of equality of opportunity is obtained if 'equality in and before the law' is replaced by '*equality in and before the society's social contract*'. This stronger version is needed to get rid of things like glass ceilings and subconscious racism. But even this is not *real* equality of opportunity. Real equality of opportunity exists when, and only when, the choices available to equally qualified people are *equally open to them as practical possibilities, and always have been*.

1.8. Measuring Social Demand

The level of social demand is not measurable precisely, because social goods have no market value. But economic demand is an objectively determinable quantity, and is therefore easier to estimate. We could, I suppose, try to estimate social demand by working out the cost of satisfying it sufficiently to enable a person to live with dignity, and provide adequately for him or herself and his or her dependents, where he or she currently lives, and tot up the costs of that person's upbringing, including his or her schooling, medical treatment, food, and so on. And, in this way, we might draw a social map of Australia, and work out a standard minimum wage for each area. Then one might add, the costs of all of the nation's government institutions, agencies, and social programs, including all of the nation's governments, legal institutions, armed forces (police and military), universities, research institutes, public schools and so on. And, with a bit of ingenuity, and some fudging, one might come up with a reasonable estimate of the cost to the nation of providing adequately for people's human rights, and giving them the support they would need to live with dignity in our own society.

In my view, this is how we should begin developing a strategy for the satisfaction of social demand. For this should enable us to arrive at a determinate level of social support for those who are currently unemployed, and indicate clearly where the required services are most urgently needed. It would also allow us to direct a targeted employment program, with a view to minimizing the levels of government support that are needed.

It is well known that economic demand is regionally dependent. Those regions with the greatest wealth can exercise the greatest demand. But the social demand for required goods and services must arise more from the relatively poor regions, where the need for social services is greater. The neoliberal conception of the role of government in society is therefore bound to favor the rich and richly located people at the expense of the poor and poorly located. And it is bound to favor the ready-availability of personal services to those who can easily afford them at the expense of personal services to those who cannot afford them.

One would expect to find that the need for social services is concentrated in specific towns and suburbs. The needs for housing, employment, public transport, drug treatment and rehabilitation, aged care, and so on, are all likely to be greatest in those towns or suburbs that have suffered most from high unemployment (due, for example, to factory closures, or racial vilification). Moreover, these are the locations where people are most under stress. So, it is where we are likely to find high drug addiction rates, more obesity, more unwanted pregnancies, more mental illnesses, and more youth suicides.

The need for low or semi-skilled work is also likely to be concentrated in the depressed townships and suburbs of the nation. But the kinds of employment likely to be favored economically are precisely those that people living in depressed communities are unlikely to be able to do. It is all very well to say that the capitalist processes of creative destruction will always lead to the creation of new jobs. Most innovations have hidden costs, and major innovations major costs. But, for the most part, these costs will be borne by those whose livelihoods have been destroyed by these innovations. And, the new industries, which are created in the process, are unlikely to be created at the same locations, and the skills of the displaced workers are unlikely to match the requirements of the newly created positions. Of course, some people will be retrainable, but most mature-aged workers will not be. Or, even if they were, their prospects of reemployment would be slim. Or, even if their prospects of reemployment were high, the locations of the retraining centres might well be too remote, or the jobs for which they would become fitted, not offered locally.

The neoliberal tool-kit includes no way of responding adequately to any of these social demands. Lowering interest rates to stimulate investment to increase national economic growth, which is standard neoliberal policy, may not only fail to address the problems of unemployment or underemployment; it could even be the very opposite of what is needed. Reducing interest rates to less than 3% would also seem to be pointless. It will not be likely to increase consumption of the kinds of goods and services provided by those who are about to lose their jobs. To create the kind of growth in the kinds of areas where it is needed, we need to adopt a strategy of targeting it to the kinds of developments that are needed and appropriate for those areas.

In summary, *economic demands*, which are measured by how much people (or firms) are prepared to pay for the goods or services they want, are not the same as people's *social demands*. Nor is there any reason to suppose that what is demanded economically will be either sustainable or morally sound. However, people's social demands are measured by how much they need the social goods they do not have. *And, the greater their need, the stronger the moral case for meeting them.* If, nevertheless, people are denied the goods or services they really need, just so that those who can afford to buy what they want can do so, then that too is immoral. Morally, therefore, social demand should always trump economic demand.

This is the neoliberal dilemma that young people today have to live with. For, a neoliberal society must always, by its nature, give priority to the needs and aspirations of wealthy people. For they are the ones who can, and do, exercise most economic demand. But the poor in a neoliberal society cannot muster enough economic demand to satisfy even their own basic needs, or make others sufficiently aware of what their needs are. Tens of thousands of people have to sleep rough in Australia today. And many more are chronically unemployed. This imbalance is not only distressing and destructive, it is also morally wrong, a moral scar on our society, which has many highly undesirable consequences, which affect particularly the lives of those who are the victims of these injustices.

PART II

THE PROBLEMS OF NEOLIBERALISM

2.1. Debt and Unemployment

Australia has chronic problems with unemployment and sky-rocketing private debt. The two problems are linked, and both, I will argue, were creations of the neoliberal reform policies begun in Australia in the 1980s. They are linked, because the aim of the reform policy was to shift the balance of power in the community from the instruments of government to those of business, or, where this is impractical, to making the instruments of government behave as much like corporations as possible. The underlying reasons behind this movement were the beliefs (a) that powerful governments are, by their nature, oppressive, and (b) that business enterprises are the original and most proficient creators of wealth, opportunity, and facility for the citizens of all modern societies.[8]

The period that began with the elections of Margaret Thatcher (1979), and Ronald Reagan (1981) as the heads of their respective governments, and ended abruptly with the global financial crisis of 2008 is known as 'the neoliberal era'.

But things have not worked out as neoliberal theorists had hoped. The problem of unemployment has become a serious one, because no neoliberal society in the world has been able to provide adequate employment opportunities for all of the people it was intended to serve. Full employment, it seems, can be approached only in boom times, but evidently it cannot be sustained. On the contrary, every boom seems likely to be followed by a prolonged period of economic stagnation, with high, and often crippling, levels of unemployment.

Household debt has also become a serious problem for neoliberalism. For no neoliberal society has been able to create high enough levels of employment, without simultaneously encouraging people to go heavily into debt. This was certainly the experience of the neoliberal era in Australia, and it appears to have been the experience of the whole neoliberal world in the thirty years leading up to the Global Financial Crisis (GFC). The citizens of neoliberal Europe were urged by their governments to keep on spending—as if their credit-worthiness had no limits. But the exponentially increasing levels of private debt in the boom periods were clearly unsustainable. Moreover, the greater the level of household debt, the more it acquired the nature of public debt, since no government that had encouraged its citizens to spend so lavishly, but also wished to retain their support, could possibly allow its banks to fail, and its citizens to face mass bankruptcy. The banks would have to be bailed out, or nationalized, if they had lent too much, and people had begun to panic.

Australia, like the rest of the capitalist world also has a growing problem with inequality. A high degree of inequality may be tolerable in a society where the poor can reasonably hope for a better future. But, while times have been good for the rich, such hope is rapidly being extinguished for the poor. The wealthiest people in rich societies like ours live on incomes measured in tens of millions of dollars, and are the owners of nearly all of the means of production, distribution, information and exchange. And the top quintile of salary earners is also very wealthy. But the statistics are obscene. In Australia, for example, 'the seven richest individuals hold more wealth than the 1.73 million households in the bottom 20 per cent'[9]. And, Australia's income and wealth inequality is much less than disparities that can be found in the US, and in much of Europe. So, for the poor, it is like the Depression all over again. As Joseph Stiglitz (2012) argues, this is a recipe for disaster.

However, I do not wish to discuss the consequences of gross inequality here. Stiglitz has done this much better than I can. My focus will be on the consequences of the huge amount of private debt that our society has accumulated, mostly during John Howard's prime-ministership, and the unsustainably high levels of unemployment that our society has had for almost the whole of the neoliberal era. My aim is to explore alternative strategies for achieving and maintaining full employment, and one of these has certainly been to encourage people to borrow money, in order to bet on rising prices in the housing and share markets. This strategy got unemployment down to just 4.0% at the end of the Howard era—the lowest it had been since the early seventies.[10]

To solve the problems created by private debt and unemployment, I believe it will be necessary to revisit this old social model, the welfare state, and relearn the strategy of targeting growth to create full employment. The neoliberal strategy of just stimulating economic growth is effectively just one of leaving it to business enterprises to decide for themselves what they want to do. But business enterprises will never consciously seek to eliminate unemployment. It is not in their DNA. And, they are highly unlikely to achieve this result just by accident. They are responsive to economic demand. But they are basically insensitive to social demand. Therefore, unless those who need our support socially are in a position to make their demands economically, they will either not be met at all, or, if they are ineligible for support under some government program, then they will have to be met by charity, or by an emergency grant.

Australia's welfare state, and its post-war development under Ben Chifley and Sir Robert Menzies, certainly had its faults. But they were mostly social faults, which were common at the time. White Australia policy, gender role-casting, blatant protectionism, environmental neglect, animal cruelty, and the social exclusion of minorities (gays, lesbians, and some ethnic minorities) were all among our *socially inherited* traits at that time, and similar faults are to be found in most European and former colonial societies in the 1950s and 60s. So, please don't blame Australia's welfare state for these defects. The members of most Western societies in the post-war years were prone to such socially divisive attitudes, but welfare states no more so than most other kinds of states.

Nor is the threat of anthropogenic climate change one that can be laid at the feet of the welfare state. It is a serious problem, which requires urgent action. But prosperous nations everywhere, and of every political color, contributed to its creation, and none is uniquely fitted to deal with it. Naomi Kline (2014) has argued that the selfishness of capitalism got us into this mess, and has systematically been blocking moves to cope with it. No doubt it has. But my case for revisiting the welfare state does not depend on this thesis. It depends upon the intractable problems of debt, social inequality and chronic unemployment, which are occurring everywhere in the neoliberal world. And these problems would still exist, even if there were no problem at all of anthropogenic climate change.

2.2. The Neoliberal Strategy

The neoliberal strategy for dealing with unemployment has been to stimulate economic growth, but to avoid steering it. One can either reduce interest rates, they say, or offer tax concessions that are to be paid for by cutting government programs. But neoliberals believe we should always, if possible, leave it to businesses to decide what they want to do. That is their job, and that is how a free society works.

In every capitalist society, there must be a kind of inverse relationship between its economic growth rate (GDP) and its level of unemployment. For GDP measures business activity, and the greater the level of business activity, the more people must be employed. Therefore, they say, if we want full employment, we must seek to achieve a level of growth sufficient to bring this about, whatever direction might be chosen. And, in general, it is true that the higher the growth rate, the lower the unemployment rate, and conversely. Therefore, a strategy for stimulating growth should increase the availability of work, if we push it hard enough. But why should we leave it to businesses to decide the direction in which we should try to move the overall economy?

Without direction, high rates of growth in the economy are evidently required for anything like full employment to be achieved. But these rates of growth have proven to be unsustainable. For they can be achieved, it seems, only if consumers spend much more than they earn on local production, and keep on doing so.

It will be argued, however, that while GDP may be a good measure of overall business activity in any society, boosting it to create full employment is a very blunt instrument to use. For increasing the GDP may not do much towards creating full employment. Firstly, it may not succeed in producing any more jobs in the regions where many people are out of work. Secondly, it may not succeed in producing *the kinds* of jobs that we must create if we are to compete with our trading partners in the various FTAs of which we are members. Most of Australia's unemployed live in the depressed suburbs of big cities, or in country towns, and the unemployed workers in these areas have already lost their jobs due to international competition. Thirdly, the growth stimulus strategy will not succeed in training anyone to do the kind of work we must do more efficiently than any of our trading partners, if we are to remain prosperous.

We may also have worries about the effectiveness of some growth strategies. It is true that decreasing interest rates will normally increase borrowing, and so increase both spending and business activity, and hence the GDP. But if interest rates are already down to below 3%, there is no reason to believe that decreasing them further will significantly increase economic activity. When interest rates get that low, it is business confidence that needs to be boosted, and reducing interest rates further is usually a sign that the demand for goods and services is chronically low, and therefore a bad time for businesses to be expanding production. So, it is probably just wishful thinking to suppose that reducing interest rates below 3% will significantly increase economic activity.

What the government must do, in such circumstances, is try to stimulate employment in a targeted way, and set about enacting measures that will increase demand in those places in which employment is most needed. It does not have to be an *overall* growth strategy. It just needs to be a *well-targeted* one—to provide opportunities for all who need jobs. It also needs to be *sustainable*. That is, the strategy must be geared to providing for needs that are on-going, not to ones that are satisfiable in the short term (unless society happens to have a lot of such needs), or which would require an unsustainable drain on our (or the world's) finite resources.

We might, to start with, increase unemployment benefits substantially for all of the longer-term unemployed people in the country, with the aim of bringing their incomes up to the level of the old-age pension, or thereabouts. For these people will almost certainly be the most difficult ones to provide employment for. Many will now need long-term support and training before they can be returned to the active workforce.

This would, apparently, be well-targeted spending. It would put money directly into the hands of the chronically unemployed, wherever they might live, and so stimulate demand in all of these areas. Probably, most of those to whom this money is provided, would be found to be living in poverty-stricken areas, which themselves are in need of extra support. So, it would be seen by many, and even by many other unemployed people, as fair, because the long-term unemployed have suffered the indignity of unemployment for the longest time. Indeed, they are the primary victims of the neoliberal era, and the social ills it has inevitably created. Chronically unemployed people hardly existed in the post-war welfare state, when unemployment averaged just two percent. These are the levels of unemployment we must now aim for.

But this move would be just a start. For, in the longer term, the poverty-stricken areas of the cities and countryside will all need more local business activities in their own regions. And, if we were just to raise the long-term unemployment pension to the old-age pension, that would provide the chronically unemployed with the dignity of money, and enable them to live a more normal life in their own communities. To fully restore their self-respect, which is now an uphill battle, they really need a job that will pay them a living wage. And, in my view, it must be the task of every government in a first-world country to provide enough work, so that everyone is able to live with dignity in their home community. That is the hope, and the message, of the *Universal Declaration of Human Rights*.

If the experience of the Europeans is anything to go by, full employment will not be achieved by the standard neoliberal strategies. Lowering interest rates will not do it. Nor will reducing taxation on the wealthy, or cutting expenditure on social services. These strategies have been tried and failed. But there is nothing else in the neoliberal cupboard. Consequently, unemployment remains high everywhere in Europe, just as it has been consistently in Australia since the mid-seventies. It may be true that increasing taxes, raising interest rates, and increasing expenditure on existing social services would all have the opposite effect on business activity, and throw more people out of work. But if interest rates are not actively discouraging people from expanding their business activities, there is no point in making them any lower.

It has always been obvious that nations cannot keep on growing forever, unless the growth pattern asymptotes to zero. But without radically changing the way that goods and services are distributed in most societies today, zero growth would almost certainly lead to disaster. Therefore, we need to think carefully before we embrace a low or zero growth strategy. And, I do not propose to urge such a strategy here. Nevertheless, it may be possible to achieve a pattern of growth that is at once:

(a) sufficient for people's wellbeing, and our national social agenda,

(b) well-directed to what people need, and

(c) provides for overall near-zero, or even negative, economic growth.

For the absolute level of economic growth is not, in itself, a relevant consideration in the evaluation of a social policy. If an economy is growing in every sector in which we want it to grow, but declining in every way we want it to decline,[11] then that is overall a pretty good outcome, even if the GDP is not increasing. And such an outcome is, I believe, a possible one. Moreover, if it leads to *full employment* with little or no economic growth, which I believe is also possible, then that would be a very good outcome indeed, because it could well be sustainable—even in the long term.

In this part of the essay, we will be concerned with the targeting of economic growth for the coming age. I cannot say whether or not it would lead to a sustainable outcome. But I cannot see any good reason why it should not do so. I will focus specifically on the question of how to correct for the distortions created by the neoliberal economy of my own country, Australia. Australia is a fairly average sort of capitalist society, not so big and rich that it is able to dominate world markets, or so small and powerless that it is strategically unimportant. So, what I have to say should be directly relevant to countries with similar political and economic profiles, but only indirectly relevant to rich and powerful countries, like the USA or China, or poor and impoverished ones, such as Bangladesh or Myanmar.

I will begin by discussing what might be politically possible in Australia, given its recent history and its long-standing traditions. For there is little point in trying to develop a program for creating full employment, which could not possibly be implemented.

2.3. Natural Social Conservatism

Social conservatism exists in all societies, but in democracies it is largely determinative of what is politically possible. It limits what democratic governments are able to do in their existing circumstances, without loss of power. In dictatorships, I suppose, almost anything is possible. A dictator could even transform his/her society into a democracy by decree, by developing a carefully prepared program of establishing democratic institutions. But there is little point in discussing the capabilities of dictatorships, since, given their history, no one in his or her right mind would want to live in one. It is, however, important to consider the national capabilities of stable governments that are ruled with the consent and support of their people.

It does not matter whether the societies they govern are, strictly speaking, democracies. Philosophically, it depends only on the degree to which they are answerable to their people. On the one hand, a political party, that enjoys the support of some very powerful organisations, might technically be a democratic one. But such a party would not necessarily be answerable primarily to the people. It might only be answerable to the powerful organisations that support it. On the other hand, it is possible for the government of a one-party state to listen to, and consult effectively, with its electorate, even if it is not technically a democracy. We should not, for example, be too hasty in judging China, which has about a seventh of the world's population, and has had to deal with huge problems of poverty and lack of developed infrastructure.

The national capabilities of the governments of democratically responsive societies normally depend on their recent histories (say the last 30 years). For this is the period in which the most politically aware adults in any normal community have themselves experienced. These years are therefore likely to have been the formative ones politically for a great many people. But people brought up in any society are also likely to be aware of, and to appreciate, some of its long-standing traditions, which may surface to become politically relevant in times of crisis. In Australia, these traditions include a limited, but otherwise strongly egalitarian form of social humanism (Evatt and Chifley) on the left,[12] and an Empire conservative form of social liberalism (Menzies) on the right. In China, there is the ancient tradition of Confucianism, which is still very influential. In the US, there are significant traditions predating the Civil War of 150 years ago (the Tea Party, deep racial prejudice), which have re-emerged, because of a crisis of confidence in American values. This crisis was, I believe, created by the disastrous wars in Vietnam, Iraq and Afghanistan, the GFC, and the election of a black socially liberal President. In Britain, the betrayal of Labour values by Labour governments in the neoliberal era rekindled both Scottish nationalism and the spirit of 1945, and brought about the election of Jeremy Corbyn as leader of the British Labour Party. Such traditions tend to re-emerge in times of crisis, when old people, who are normally the keepers and spokespersons for the old traditions, re-emerge as significant political players.

We are now, I think, in such a time of crisis, not only in Australia, but in most other countries in the Western world. And it is now appropriate to consider what might be politically possible, given our neoliberal core conservatism, and our historical traditions.

In this age of plenty, it is likely that many, if not most, mature adults in prosperous neoliberal societies such as Australia have plenty of everything they need, and most of the things they have ever wanted. Moreover, people in this category have probably been able to *do* most of the things that they have ever really wanted to do. So, for these people, neoliberalism appears to have served them well. For many others of this age group, things may not be quite so good. But the wealthier of them are still likely to be much better off today than they remember being when they were young. So, naturally, neoliberalism has a strong and dedicated following among the relatively rich people of mature-age in most neoliberal societies. It certainly has in Australia, and it is the dominating political philosophy of both of the major parties.

People who are now in the fifties and sixties constitute the socially conservative core in Australia. They are generally known as the 'baby-boomers'. For the poor, under-educated, chronically unemployed, and the technologically displaced blue-collar workers, the opposite is the case. They will probably look back on the neoliberal era as a period of devastation, impoverishment, and loss of hope for a better future. As Dennis Glover's recent book so clearly illustrates, the families living and working in the decaying industrial suburbs of Melbourne have never had it so bad since the days of the Great Depression. But they are a minority. And, they are largely forgotten or ignored by most of the socially conservative core.

Socially conservative cores also exist in many subcultures of stable societies. Indeed, every major subsection of a stable society is likely to have its own socially conservative core. Those who belong in such stable groups, when they do not have to, presumably find some satisfaction in doing so. There is a conservative core of Liberal voters in Australia, and of Republican voters in America. And, there is also a conservative core of Labor voters in Australia, of Labour in the UK, and of Democrats in America. Core conservatism is thus an attitude of mind, rather than political position. It is an attitude born of the ways of thinking and behaving that are thought to have been successful in the past for the people of a given social group. In China, most members of the Communist Party (the CPC) today are probably, in this sense, core conservatives.

The existence of large blocks of core conservative attitudes is not always a good thing. For such blocks can sometimes present democratic barriers to much-needed social reforms. If the circumstances in which people are living should change, or, alternatively, if the circumstances should turn out to be much more damaging than they were earlier thought to be, then those who have been living well, and in blissful ignorance of the approaching storm, are likely to react strongly to deny any political demands for change that would affect the conservatives of that group. Such, it seems, was the reaction of many people in Australia and elsewhere to the steady build-up of CO_2 in the atmosphere, and the need to set a limit to it. It was also, as Steven Keen (2001, 2011) has argued persuasively, the reaction of most mainstream professional economists to the Global Financial Crisis. They remained wedded to their neoclassical models of the capitalist societies they served, despite the fact that none of them was able to predict its coming.

This kind of core conservatism is less common in the sciences than in social theory, because the methodology of science requires that scientific theories be tested empirically, and that any adverse findings be adequately accounted for in subsequent theory. But there is core conservatism even in the sciences. As Thomas Kuhn (1962) argued, scientific revolutions in the empirical sciences normally take a generation or more to become widely accepted in the scientific community. Frequently, the defenders of earlier theories fight a kind of rearguard action, and try desperately to hold on to the positions they have always held, and in some cases

have significantly contributed to. In areas of research that are morally, politically or culturally sensitive, scientific revolutions may take even longer.

There is no denying that economics is sensitive in all of these ways. So, it would not be unreasonable to expect radically new economic theories to take many generations to become widely accepted by professional economists, even if the new explanations of economic phenomena that become available at the cutting edge are manifestly superior to any that can be provided using the older theories. But resistance to radical change in economic theory has become scandalous, as Steven Keen, for one, has been arguing for twenty years or more.

2.4. Defending the Indefensible

After the 1929 market crash, which had not been anticipated, and seemed to come from nowhere, one would have expected some fundamental theoretical changes in economic theory. One would, at least, have expected a convincing analysis of what went wrong, of why it was not anticipated, and a well-considered program to ensure that such a thing never happens again. But no such analysis was ever forthcoming from within the neoclassical economic establishment. For, as we can now see with hindsight, it was the neoclassical theory of money, which blinded them to the symptoms of the disease. For, according to this tradition, money is not real wealth. Consequently, they accept a Neutral Money hypothesis, according to which money is not capital, but just a token of capital possession. Consequently, it was argued, people who borrow money, are not borrowing capital. They are only borrowing tokens of capital, e.g. in order to effect some real

55

exchange of goods and services. It is, of course, very convenient to have money, because the old barter system of the pre-moneyed economies, did not allow complex exchanges of goods and services of the kinds we now take for granted. But, fundamentally, they say, the real exchanges in commerce are all just exchanges of goods and services. Money is only a *facilitator* of this process, which enables us to select the best and most economical producers of such goods or services simply by paying money for them.

According to neoclassical theory, people who have lots of money have a large store of wealth, and that is its sole value—as a store of wealth. But Keynes (1937) rejected this thesis as absurd. This is what he said in dismissing it:

> But in the world of the classical economy, what an insane use to which to put it [i.e. money]! For it is a recognised characteristic of money as [just] a store of wealth that it is barren; whereas practically every other form of storing wealth yields some interest or profit. Why should anyone outside a lunatic asylum wish to use money [just] as a store of wealth? (Keen, 2001: 210)

Keynes argues that *the monetary unrealism of neoclassical economics blinds them to the important role that money has in the real economy of a country*. For it instructs economists to ignore money, and to think only in terms of concrete wealth and changes in wealth. For example, neoclassical economists argue that private debt must, in the long run, be economically irrelevant.[13] For, one agent's debt must always be another's asset; so, they must ultimately cancel one another.[14] Consequently, neoclassical economists rarely take much notice of levels of private debt. They are interested in the extent of *government* indebtedness, because this must be an investment of national wealth, and, in all democra-

cies, people want to know how their government's revenues are being spent. But, from a neoclassical point of view, the extent of *private indebtedness* (as measured by the private debt PD/GDP ratio of a society) is not a very interesting figure.

But, it turns out that PD/GDP is a very interesting figure. For it has enabled non-classical economists to predict severe economic downturns in capitalist economies. The reason for this is simple: In normal times ponzi schemes are shunned, because, as everyone knows, the price bubble will eventually burst, and those who have bought into the scheme on the promise of future gains, but have not yet realised upon their investments, will soon be caught, and find themselves holding only worthless pieces of paper. Such schemes operating on a national scale may not be possible in neoclassical perfect markets, because all investors in such markets are supposedly perfectly rational, as well as perfectly knowledgeable, about the quality of the investments they are making. But real investors have neither of these perfections. Mostly, they invest in shares or real estate, not because of the rents or dividends they expect to receive, and pay tax on, but more because of the capital gains they hope to make quickly, and on which they will pay less tax.

Australia's long term private debt to GDP ratio

Fisher & Kent 1999; RBA Historical Data; Tables D02, G12

Figure 1

This graph (Figure 1) showing the PD/GDP ratio since 1860 is quite remarkable. It shows the period of extraordinary prosperity in the build-up to the great depression of the 1890s, the euphoria that preceded the great depression of the 1930s, and finally the enthusiasm for economic reform in the 1980s, leading up to the 'recession we had to have, in of the 1991-2, followed by the debt led housing and share booms of the Howard years, which preceded the crash of 2008. It also shows the extraordinary lack of private indebtedness in the welfare state era, from 1945 to 1975.

In most circumstances, the practice of borrowing money to make money is commendable. This is the standard way to grow a business. But when people are buying things just because they believe that their purchases will increase in value over time, whatever they do, then you have what is in essence a ponzi scheme. And, when pursued by thousands of investors, it can easily turn into a sort of national ponzi scheme. For, the rising prices of the finite stocks of shares or properties being purchased (due to increasing investment), may well be taken as indicating that these items are becoming more and more valuable.

If they have indeed become more valuable, due to changing circumstances (more people, changing technology, improved transport facilities, etc.),[15] then these stocks may quite properly be used to fund increasing investments. But, if increasing demand is also fuelling further increases of demand, then there exists a positive feedback mechanism helping to generate higher and higher prices, which is in essence a ponzi scheme. And, if increasing prices become accepted by the banks as increasing mortgage values, then you may not only have a slow-motion ponzi scheme, you may have one that is being driven by the banks themselves in their search for profits.

The PD/GDP ratio of a society is interesting, because it can easily reveal the existence of positive feedback mechanisms in the nation's trading, when speculative borrowing is most likely to occur. Prolonged and highly significant speculative borrowing spurts, leading to exponential growth in household debt have occurred three times in Australian history—in the 1880s, the 1920s and the Howard years. In each case, the graph of the PD/GDP ratio has the ever-steepening curve that is characteristic of exponential growth, followed by a period of prolonged decline[16] of the kind one may expect in a depression.

According to Steven Keen (2011), who is one of the very few economists in the world to have predicted the GFC, and its subsequent echo in China in 2015, we are already in the first great depression of the 21st century. But neoclassical economists, like their 1920s counterparts, did not see it coming. The sky-rocketing PD/GDP ratios were not even on their radar. And, they would probably not have grasped their real significance, if they had been. For, after all, a private debt is just a couple of mutually cancelling book entries, and of no real significance, according to their outdated theory. Our Australian economists would have thought that it simply does not matter how much we owe to Chinese banks. For the credits in the Chinese accounts must balance the debits in ours. So, according to their trusted theory, all must be well. But really, it does matter, because it indicates that a national ponzi scheme has been operating in Australia, and that the credits in the Chinese banks, corresponding to our debits, will not be coming back to us through any future sales of the real estate we have bought with them.

I cannot say what neoclassical economists thought of these PD/GDP graphs, which had much the same shape everywhere in the neoliberal world. Every scientist I have shown them to sees them at once as being indicative of positive feedback mechanisms creating peaks of activity. But neoclassical economists tend to rely upon different graphs—ones that show only 'real' variables, such as GDP growth or unemployment. And, there are no indications of exponential growth of anything in any of these other graphs that would cause alarm. On the contrary, GDP is shown as increasing fairly steadily throughout the boom, accelerating a bit, perhaps, but not by much. And, unemployment is shown as falling fairly steadily, right up to the time of the GFC, and back to a fairly successful 4% or so. So, for those who turn a blind eye to Private Debt, and focus on the so-called 'real' variables, the signs were all good.

In the revised edition of his book (2011), Keen remarks:

> It may astonish non-economists to learn that conventionally trained economists ignore the role of credit and private debt in the economy—and frankly, it is astonishing. But it is the truth. Even today, only a handful of the most rebellious of mainstream 'neoclassical' economists—people like Joe Stiglitz and Paul Krugman—pay any attention to the role of private debt in the economy, and even they do so from the perspective of an economic theory in which money and debt play no intrinsic role. An economic theory that ignores the role of money and debt in a market economy cannot possibly make sense of the complex, monetary, credit-based economy in which we live. Yet this is the theory that has dominated economics for the last half century. If the market economy is to have a future, this widely believed but inherently delusional model has to be jettisoned. (pp. 57-8)

And there is no doubt that Keen (2011) is right about this. Writing in 2004, the Federal Reserve Bank's chairman Ben Bernanke saw only two decades of achievement. He did not perceive any threat. He asserted that there had been:

> not only significant improvements in economic growth and productivity but also a marked reduction in economic volatility, both in the United States and abroad, a phenomenon that has been dubbed 'the Great Moderation'.

> Recessions have become less frequent and milder, and quarter-to-quarter volatility in output and employment has declined significantly as well.

> The sources of the Great Moderation remain somewhat controversial, but as I have argued elsewhere, there is evidence for the view that improved control of inflation has contributed in important measure to *this welcome change in the economy.* (p. 65. Keen's emphases)

But Keen was in no doubt about what was happening. The PD/GDP ratio was accelerating upwards out of control, a sure sign that a national ponzi scheme, engineered and supported by the banks in search of profits, was well and truly in progress, and he said so in the final chapter of the first edition of his book, published in 2001.

2.5. Growth Strategies and Free Trade Agreements

Neoliberals argue that to overcome the problem of unemployment it is necessary to promote growth. But there are limits to what can be achieved by promoting growth in a neoliberal society. First, one can seek to reduce interest rates. But when official interest rates get down to three percent or less, and yet the problem remains unresolved, this strategy becomes self-defeating. Foreign investment dries up, and households already heavily in debt are inclined to believe that the best investment they can make is to reduce their levels of indebtedness.

A second strategy is to offer inducements to entrepreneurs to invest more. For example, a government may either reduce taxes for the wealthy (e.g. on superannuation contributions), or offer trade-offs between tax reductions and investments (e.g.

by allowing negative gearing). But these measures are not only unfair; they are also likely to lead to increasing levels of private indebtedness, as they did catastrophically in Australia between 2000 and 2008.

The strategy that is most in favour today is that of negotiating Free Trade Agreements (FTAs) with other like-minded countries. For these agreements can easily be sold as huge boosts to any nation's economy, and so, by implication, for employment. An FTA with the CUS (which is an imaginary great power such as China or the US) can easily be sold as opening up an immense new market for imports, exports, tourism, manufactures, education, agriculture, coal, iron ore, sheep, cattle, and so on. And, most people would find it very hard to argue against this. I do not propose to do so here. But it is not at all clear what would be best for Australia socially or economically in the long term. There will, presumably, be more jobs available for some of the exporters of goods and services, and fewer jobs in areas where our trading partners can supply the transportable goods and services we want, and do so more cheaply than we can supply them for ourselves. And, it must increase substantially the total *volume of trade* that occurs between the CUS and Australia. However, an FTA can also be hazardous. For an FTA may not, necessarily, increase the total volume of *trade that is in our long-term interests.* Inevitably, it will make some things economically less attractive to manufacture in Australia, and some markets much larger.

To evaluate an FTA, one must consider the three categories of goods and services that might be involved, and also the legalities (such a copyrights and litigation rights). The three categories are *transportable goods* (raw materials, manufactures), *active services* (education, tourism, entertainment), and *investment opportunities* (loans, land, housing, businesses, infrastructure projects, etc). The three are not, perhaps, exhaustive of all possibilities, or mutually exclusive. But they are adequate for the purposes of this essay.

Ideally, the negotiators of a free trade agreement should consider these three categories of trade, and decide for each which items to include or exclude, or attach any restrictions, or specify any exemptions, that may be thought to be necessary. The negotiators must consider whether the document is fair, and sufficiently in the interests of both sides to be worth pursuing. But, the fundamental questions to ask are those concerning the rights of the participating nations, their traders, their investors, and their workforces.

The main issues all revolve around those of national sovereignty. For, my chief worry about FTAs is that they are not what they appear to be. They appear to be just free trade agreements entered into voluntarily to increase trade and prosperity all around. But, in reality, they may be strategic moves to tie nations together in trading networks, which is exclusive of rival nations, but binding on them. In which case, there is a fundamental problem with FTAs. Do we want to be bound in this way? And do we want the excluded nations to be excluded?

No nation should sign an FTA for the economic benefit it promises, only to find that its national sovereignty has been compromised. Plausibly, hegemonic powers, such as the CUS, never have to worry about such things. No small or middle-sized nation could possibly pose a severe threat to the sovereignty of a great power, such as the CUS. But the CUS could easily pose a significant threat to the sovereignty of a minor partner, such as Australia, without even intending to. If, somehow, corporations registered in the CUS obtained significant ownership and control of some of the principal means of production, distribution, communication, or exchange in Australia, then Australia's sovereignty would be threatened, as indeed it has been by the Murdoch Press, whose founder was Australian by birth, but is now a US citizen. Rupert Murdoch sees himself as a king-maker, and, as his power has grown, he has shown no reluctance to use it to his own advantage, and hence to promote his US interests.

I speculate that, without global regulation to protect basic industries in small countries, all FTAs with great powers will pose threats to the independence of smaller nations. The unemployment problem, for example, probably cannot be solved politically in a neoliberal world. It surely would have been solved by now, if it were possible. It may be necessary, therefore, to work towards the development of a new international trade agreement that would prevent any hegemonic power from surrounding itself with economically dependent states, which are not bound by common idealism, but rather by free trade deals that basically serve the strategic interests of that power. Indeed, this seems to me to be precisely the battle-ground upon which the conflicting ideologies of the great powers of this world will be fought out. For, it seems to me that the TPP, which includes the USA, Japan, Canada, Australia, Chile, Singapore, Brunei, New Zealand, Peru, Malaysia, Mexico, and Vietnam is not just a trading deal. It is a powerful economic and political alliance, which is intended to counter the emerging economic power of China.

The social/moral case for signing up to such agreements is

very thin. If one is a neoliberal, then the argument for joining up may not depend as much on the benefits that the agreement will bestow on Australia. For, its real aim is to lock us in to the failed policy framework of neoliberalism, by tying us firmly into a free-trade network that is inspired by neoliberal philosophy. We can be sure that it is not going to create full employment in Australia. On the contrary, it seems likely to lead to fewer low-tech jobs, more unemployment, and an even starker divide between rich and poor.

But, perhaps I am wrong about this. FTAs can be anything from very good to very bad for businesses in each of the three categories (transportable goods, active services, and investment opportunities). For Australia, they are mostly very good for raw materials (iron ore, coal, woodchips), food grains (wheat, oats, barley, sugar), and meat (cattle, sheep, fish), where large-scale production processes (open cut mining, broad acre grazing, and mega-farming) tend to favor Australia. But they are mostly very bad for the manufacture of complex transportable goods (cars, trucks, white goods, clothing, shoes, processed foods), which favor nations with cheaper workforces, or highly automated industries enjoying huge advantages of scale, as, presumably, the CUS does. So, I see a lot more to be lost in the field of transportable goods, than there is to be gained. But perhaps we can make up for these losses in the areas of active services and investment opportunities. I doubt it. Better investment opportunities always favor the very rich to the merely rich, and the merely rich to the poor. So, the only question is whether there is sufficient benefit for us in the field of active services (tourism, education, cultural exchange, and so on). Perhaps there is. I do not know.

But there are other dangers. Becoming dependent on our trading partners is one thing. Losing the capacity to fend for ourselves is another. Yet, both may well be involved. Australia's long-term viability as a nation requires that we retain basic expertise and competence in all strategically important areas of production, distribution, information, and exchange, and continue to operate successfully in all of these areas. For, if we retain insufficient capacity for constructive work in these areas in future, we just may not be able to pick up from where we left off, (say 25 years before), if catastrophic events should make it necessary now (25 years later) to do so.

Thus, if we lose any of these competences, then we may well lose our independence for a different sort of reason. We may, over time, become *intrinsically* incapable of providing adequately for ourselves. We may simply lack the expertise. And, if this should happen in a strategically important area, then we should both (a) be laying ourselves open to industrial blackmail, and (b) to the possibility of becoming dysfunctional in some fundamental way. A new world war, for example, or a catastrophic downturn in the world economy, could throw us back on to our own resources, whatever our trade agreements may be. But if, through FTAs, we were to lose the skills to make, manage, or repair things upon which we are vitally dependent, then we are in deep trouble as a nation. I think it has been quite irresponsible of governments to have allowed our manufacturing industries to be sacrificed.

The guiding principles concerning our rights in FTAs should, therefore, be something like these:

(1) Any FTA, to which Australia is a party, must provide that effective administrative control in all areas of the

national economy will remain, *as of right*, firmly in the hands of the Australian people.

(2) No FTA shall be considered to be binding on the government of Australia if has not considered and approved of all of its clauses.

(3) No FTA can prove to be so much to the disadvantage of Australia that it makes home production in strategically important areas unviable.

(4) No FTA should effectively lock us into pursuing a neoliberal policy at home, whether we like it or not. It must allow for the possibility that the Australian people will eventually reject the framework of neoliberalism, and seek instead to target growth, specifically to create full employment for the greater good of all of its citizens.

(5) All disputes concerning the administration of an FTA should be adjudicated by a world court set up for the purpose of handling such disputes. Corporations should not be able to sue governments. Governments are responsible only (a) to their own people, and (b) to the international community.[17]

2.6. Remodelling Society

How, then, can we deal with these problems? For, assuredly, the generation that will inherit the continuing problems of gross inequality, poverty, chronic unemployment, and household debt, which our core conservative neoliberals will leave to their children and grandchildren, will not, in due course, become the conservative core of a new and flourishing society. Rather, the new generation will be living in an era much like the one that faced the Western world at the end of World War II—a world, which was exhausted from war and depression, and were confronted with the problem of creating a new world order. Yet, they achieved that and more; they created a world order that was at once more moral, more purposeful, and much more satisfying personally than any that had preceded it. It was a world that provided real equality of opportunity[18], and in which people of all backgrounds were concerned for the wellbeing of others, and wished to enable them to live with dignity in their own cultures and societies.

The task of creating a new world order had become urgent by the end of the Second World War, because, by then, it had become evident that the old order had failed, and the threat existed that the capitalist and communist systems would ultimately give rise to yet another conflict, which would be far more devastating than anything that had ever occurred before in history. The task was made all the more urgent, because the two most powerful countries on earth not only possessed nuclear weapons, but were also diametrically opposed to one another, and saw themselves as being involved in an existential struggle for survival.

In the end, the Americans appeared to win this struggle. The historic Cold War came to an end with the fall of the Berlin wall. But, a similar existential struggle now seems to be emerging between China and the US, which is commonly seen as the beginning of a new Cold War—especially in the US. And, it is very much in our interests to put the fears that create this perception to rest. For we have a strong interest in preserving peace and security in our own region. And, I am sure that neither China nor the US wants it any other way. Conflict between these two great powers would destroy the one and only chance China is likely to get in the present century of becoming as rich and invulnerable as the US. So, the Chinese desperately want a region in which they can develop peacefully, become the dominant force, and ensure that the region of South East Asia they occupy remains peaceful and secure. They will, therefore, be very likely to resist strongly any US moves to isolate China, or to 'contain' it, as though it were a savage creature, which cannot be let loose on the world.

The Americans, on the other hand, desperately want to retain their position as the sole great power in the world, and ensure that its neoliberal ideology prevails in the battle of ideas. I do not support either of these objectives. Neoliberal ideology is, as I have been arguing here, deeply flawed, and I think there is room for a different kind of power at the summit. But I also stand opposed to Chinese authoritarianism, and would like to see a softening of the Chinese position. Specifically, I would like to see China become a democracy that is committed to establishing a strongly egalitarian society that respects the full spectrum of human rights. And, indeed, I am hopeful that this will eventually happen. Attempts to paint China as a warlike aggressive nation seem to me to be just propaganda.

Naturally, the Chinese want to control the sea-lanes in and out of China, because China is, or will soon become, the greatest trading nation in history. So containing China, and not allowing it to have control of its sea-lanes, is very dangerous, and, I believe, radically ill conceived. China has a right to protect its merchant fleet, and the merchant fleets of other nations bound to or from its ports. Piracy in the region is not just an imaginary threat. So, it is rightly concerned at the USA's pivoting to Asia, because it bears all of the hallmarks of an operation to surround China by hostile forces. Since World War II, Australia has chosen to become an American satellite. So, its strategic position is one of dependence upon the US. But the decision concerning the desirability or otherwise of collaborating with the US to contain China, should be our decision, not America's. Our interests are not the same as America's.

I am worried about America's pivoting, and, in particular, its pivoting to Asia. For I am not sure that America is dextrous enough to pivot around the world without treading on a great many toes. I don't want to be protected from China, as though it posed a threat to our security. For, it doesn't pose a threat, and it will not do so, unless it is provoked. At present, I think China would be our natural ally, if we should be threatened by any other South East Asian nations. And, it is in our interests to encourage China to think of us as a supporter of hers in the region. The American alliance, on the other hand, is a threat to our security, because it sets us at odds with Chinese ambitions to become the dominant power in the region.

Malcolm Fraser (2014) has made a case for this very powerfully in his recent book *Dangerous Allies*, where he argues that while there is no good reason why we should not have a strategic alliance (such as the ANZAC Treaty) with the US, we should be willing to allow China to develop freely into a major power.

The Chinese polity is not a democracy, because there are no opposition parties. But nor is it, any longer, a tyranny, as Hayek once defined it. Its Government rules with the support of the vast majority of its people. There is also, currently, plenty of rivalry for the top job in China. With the defeat of the 'Gang of

Four', following the disastrous 'Great Leap Forward', the threat of any new dictatorship after Mao has greatly receded. Indeed, since the embrace of Western socioeconomic strategies by Deng Xaioping in 1978, a new kind of regime has emerged to take its place—one that now appears to be a sort of Confucian adaptation of capitalism with a communist overlay. The leaders of this seemingly bizarre regime are drawn from a large, comparatively well-educated and politically sophisticated ruling elite, viz. the members of the CPC (Communist Party of China).

This new Chinese system looks a bit like a 21st century version of the Confucian ideal. Historically, Confucianism required a large public service, consisting of dedicated scholars, strategically placed throughout the realm, selected for their knowledge and talent by public exams, and committed to serving the Emperor—advising and assisting him in his administration. It is also a bit reminiscent of Plato's *Republic*. For this too had a ruling elite. The ruling elite of Plato's *Republic* were all, notionally, philosophers, or lovers of wisdom/knowledge (*episteme*). But, as the classical concept of *episteme* is explained in the writings of Plato and Aristotle, we should not think of philosophy here as being only the kind of inquiry undertaken in today's philosophy departments. Today's equivalents of Plato's philosophers would have to include nearly all of the scientifically and mathematically literate people in the community.

Plato's underlying metaphysical theory does not give much credence to his political doctrines. According to Plato, a philosophical understanding of the world is superior to any other kind of knowledge (such as that of a soldier, craftsman or artisan). For, a philosophical understanding, he said, requires knowledge of the Forms, which, he thought, were the abstract, but ontologically fundamental, templates by which the real world is structured. So, if a prince is to be the ruler of a just society, Plato argued, it is imperative that he should have knowledge of the Forms of Justice and Goodness. Accordingly, these abstract ideals are the ones that Plato discussed in his great book *The Republic*.

However, I do not think we should try to reconstruct our society, using either present-day China or Plato's *Republic* as our model. Neither would be realistic or desirable. Nor are Plato's *a priori* foundations of knowledge tenable. But we might well try to build a much fairer and more inclusive state, which resonates with our own past, and has *some* of the characteristics of these two models built into it. The idea of an army of professionally trained people distributed throughout the community, and paid to: (a) advise people of their legal/moral rights and obligations, (b) provide them with technical assistance where it is needed, (c) advise governments (local, state and national) concerning the effectiveness and/or dangers of their programs, and (d) propose alternatives, where necessary, seems to me to be entirely sensible, especially in these days of rapid social and technological change. This is perhaps one of the lessons we might learn from the Chinese experience.

Specialists might also be needed to help cope with people who have been left behind technically, as a result of the pace of change, and with the associated problems of ignorance, drug abuse, and violent behaviour. Many professionals (doctors, dentists, teachers, counsellors, and so on) are already widely distributed in the community. But with technological advances, we may need to extend the range of specialist services available, especially in the country towns, and in many of the poorer suburbs of the big cities. For example, we seem now to need thousands of mental health workers, and staff for drug treatment and rehabilitation centres, and women's refuges. And, if we don't need them yet, we almost certainly will need them soon.

The population of Australia is ageing, as are the populations of most Western nations. Nevertheless, we should, consistently with our long-standing tradition, aim to keep old people in the own homes for as long as possible. For, by all accounts, most old people find nursing home accommodation somewhat alien-ating, and would prefer to struggle along at home, for as long as they can. Our ageing population therefore bodes well for our future. The idea that it creates a burden that future generations will have to bear, is absurd. On the contrary, it offers hope, be-cause it will provide ample work, which cannot plausibly be outsourced, for future generations of people to do—the creation and maintenance of good home-based aged care facilities for all, and the education, entertainment and enjoyment of all of these older citzens. This is a source of demand that surely cannot be met by our trading partners more cheaply, or with better service. And, it is a market that is just made for local employment, be-cause it will provide employment opportunities *everywhere, and in all communities*. Some such employment will inevitably have to be subsidised. And most of it should be carefully monitored and vetted, because old people are frequently targeted by crim-inal gangs seeking to profit from them. Probably, local councils should monitor all geriatric services, and vet the applications for these kinds of jobs.

If we are to learn anything from Platonism, I think we might well be concerned with the role of rationality in the conduct of government. Plato believed in government by an educated elite. But for a social democracy, it would have to be government by the representatives of a well-informed and educated public. We should, therefore, be willing to consider creating a public education system constructed along the lines of the ABC with a mandate to present well-researched programs on scientific, social, moral and political issues. For, in a well-functioning democracy, the public has the right to be well informed about all matters of public concern. But, in Australia, and in many other countries around the world, there is now a near monopoly of ownership of all of the means of accurate and readily accessible public information. And, the owners of these private networks are now so powerful that no democratic government is ever likely to be able to challenge them successfully. They are untouchable, because, in a democracy, *the rights to freedom of speech and expression, which are naturally championed by the media giants, would always be likely to trump an individual's right to be well informed.* Institutions like the ABC are the only plausible defence a democracy has to the dominance of the media giants.

2.7. The Kind of State Required

Plausibly, the kind of state that would suit us best is one that combines the efficiency of free market economies in distributing goods and services with the productivity of a highly educated, well trained, and fully employed workforce. Historically, the kind of state that has succeeded best in satisfying these two requirements was the welfare state of the Chifley, Menzies, and Whitlam era. It was fully employed; unemployment for the thirty years from 1945 to 1975 averaged 2.0%, and exceeded 3% only briefly in 1961. Its economy grew steadily throughout the period; the average GDP growth rate from 1960 to 1974 was 5.2%. And, it employed the market mechanism to distribute goods and services, which, in times of full employment is not grossly unfair. On the other hand, the neoliberal state of 1980 to 2008 did not succeed in creating full employment. It got unemployment down to a low of 4.0% at the end of the period, just before the GFC hit, but it never succeeded in achieving anything like the low unemployment rates of the welfare state era. Its economic growth was slower than in the welfare state period, and its income tax system was also less progressive. Moreover, because of the high levels of unemployment (averaging 6.9%), and its use of a wide-spectrum consumption tax, its system for distributing goods and services was not as fair.

The current account deficit also remained at or near zero levels, so that intractable levels of foreign debt did not accumulate, as they did throughout the neoliberal era. It may have been a few million dollars in the red, or a few million in the black. But it was never so uncontrollably negative as it was throughout the whole of the neoliberal era. In fact, the Current Account was often in surplus when we had a welfare state, and we easily paid our way in the world.

By every plausible economic measure of which I am aware, the post-war welfare state in Australia was more successful than the economy of the neoliberal era. The graph on p.50 should really be turned upside down, with the negative value of private indebtedness pointing downwards. For, as Minsky rightly remarks, capitalist societies are '*unstable upwards*'. That is, they are disposed to be unstable in the directions of increasing levels of private debt and debt-fuelled affluence. The welfare state era, was the period in which we mostly paid our way in the world. And the degree of affluence that people acquired in this period was not gained at any cost to future generations. On the contrary, the welfare state created the wealth that was mortgaged by successive neoliberal governments to create the debt-fuelled affluence that we saw in the Howard years.

Nevertheless, the welfare state of this era may not, as it stands, be a useful model for the future. In an earlier publication, I argued that Labor's historic mission is to create contemporary welfare states. I still agree with this. But I fear that it will be widely misunderstood. For, the world has changed a great deal since the post-war period, and any new kind of state would have to be constructed in our present circumstances, and according to contemporary moral values. But the biggest and most important changes are irreversible. There is no going back now on the digital revolution. Nor is there any reversal of the policies of social and political inclusion either possible or desirable. We cannot go back to the gender casting of roles, or to the racism or homophobia that prevailed in this earlier period. The things we must take from the welfare state era, are its national commitments to full employment, equality of educational opportunity, and to the ideal of allowing every person to develop their full potential. We can call this a welfare state for the 21st century, if you like. But it might better be understood simply as a modern fully employed social democracy.

Australia has a long-standing tradition of social egalitarianism. And neoliberalism, which was always in danger of generating high levels of inequality, has done precisely this. It has made what was once a highly egalitarian country into one of the most unequal societies in the world. In its ACOSS report (2015): *Inequality in Australia: A Nation Divided,* the authors note:

> While substantial, the share of income received by the top 1% in Australia is not as large as in other OECD countries [the share of income going to the top 1% in the US is about double that of Australia]. However, the share going to the top 1% has been increasing faster in Australia than in some other OECD nations. In 1980, Australia had the second lowest share of any OECD country accruing to the top 1% [after Sweden], whereas we are now between fifth and seventh in the ladder. (p. 17)

This was never what the early advocates of neoliberalism promised to deliver. But it has delivered it nevertheless.

Neoliberalism also promised to deliver high quality education for all. But the neoliberal regimes that have existed since about 1980, have not done so. On the contrary, state school education has suffered dramatically, as increasingly scarce public educational resources have dried up, or been diverted to the private educational system. Many of the parents of school-aged children are desperately sending them to private schools, even if it is a major sacrifice for them to do so. So the present education system is certainly not fair. And, because of this, it is not as productive of high quality educational development as it could be.

The system of government we require for Australia must be one that allows people to pursue their educational objectives as far as their talents permit, and to fully develop their personalities as Australian citizens, just as it says in the *UDHR*. The neoliberal decision to fund private schools at the expense of public ones fails on this score too.

If these arguments are sound, then the kind of state that we must seek to construct must be, like the earlier welfare state, one that is strongly committed to egalitarianism. And, in accordance with our long-standing tradition, it should also be a state in which comparatively high levels of achievement in education, health, wealth, welfare and social security all exist. For these have existed in this country for most of its existence, and could fairly easily be restored to us now that the neoliberal era is over.[19] Rationally, the kind of social structure we need, and should aim to construct now in Australia, is a welfare state that is specifically geared to creating full, continuing and productive employment. It must be a state that sets about developing and satisfying high levels of social demand, requiring work that needs to be done by local people acting locally.

The kind of state we need to develop is one in which growth and development are targeted appropriately to the people needing jobs, in the areas near where they live, doing work that they are either capable of doing now, or could quickly learn to do in future.

2.8. The Problems to be Addressed

The market-driven economies of the world's wealthiest nations have not been able to create enough demand to create full employment—even with free trade deals. Retailers spend billions on advertising to try to generate enough demand—often for things that hardly anyone wants. They package them so that you cannot buy only what you need. You always have to buy several times what you need, and pay for the packaging, because smaller packages are simply unavailable. But the problem is not just one of marketing or packaging. There is a surfeit of production of goods, and now that the inevitable process of debt deflation[20] has begun, in the aftermath of the GFC, there is little hope that further cuts in interest rates will stimulate more investment in manufacturing.

But, such are the marketing opportunities likely to be created by the deals with Japan, China, India and South Korea, that this round of FTAs may well succeed in clearing some of the backlog of unemployed people in Australia. I hope so. But, even if it is successful, it will almost certainly be at the cost of

    (a) what remains of our old manufacturing industries,

    (b) our ownership of Australian resources, (and hence our national self-reliability), and

    (c) our responsibilities to those who have been injured by past neoliberal programs.

These are all problems that need to be dealt with. A nation without significant manufacturing industries for supplying world markets is necessarily a very dependent one. The free trade agreements we have already signed would commit us to living in a society with virtually no labour-intensive industries involved in the production of commercial goods and services. And any internationally marketable goods or services that we could possibly make in Australia, but which could be supplied by an FTA partner, will almost certainly be supplied by that partner, more cheaply than we could supply it ourselves.[21] Therefore, we must, in all of these ways, become more and more dependent upon our

FTA partners.

Moreover, a nation without significant manufacturing industries is one with only a narrow range of employment opportunities. It makes not only the unskilled, but also the traditionally skilled blue-collar workers and their female counterparts, more or less redundant. And, if they cannot be made technologically proficient, while they are still young enough to be re-employed, or made socially useful in some other way, then the range of employment opportunities available to them in a society such as ours must be become inadequate. As, indeed, it already is. The FTAs are therefore likely to result in very high unemployment rates in this group. At first, this can be expected to give rise to anger and resentment. But, in the longer term, if neoliberal philosophy prevails politically, then it is likely to turn into bitterness and frustration, and cause all of the social and mental disorders that characterise the chronically unemployed poor in all modern capitalist societies.

Finally, a nation that willingly enters into free trade agreements that are likely to cause even more people to feel cast out of any constructive role in our society must face up to the fact that the group that is most likely to be affected is the one that is already the most threatened. Consequently, the task of treating, rehabilitating, and re-engaging those who are already suffering from unemployment sickness, e.g. by becoming depressed or addicted to drugs, will probably be made all the more difficult.

Therefore, the FTA with China, which was announced at the G20 Summit recently, is not all a bed of roses. Nor is the Trans-Pacific Partnership that is now being negotiated. It demands that we put aside most of the profits arising from these deals to provide for the wellbeing of those who will suffer displacement as a result. The benefits of these deals must not be allowed to flow only to those with money to spend, while those who lose their jobs must just sit by and watch others enjoy the things for which their working lives have been sacrificed. The government has a clear moral duty to promote the wellbeing and dignity of all Australians, not just look after the already wealthy or technologically highly competent sections of our community.

On the other hand, free trade appears to have been a boon to the poor and underdeveloped countries of the world. It has lifted their productivity (as measured by GDP per capita) to unprecedented heights (Michael Spence, 2011). We should not, therefore, abandon the laudable aims of globalisation, unless we are: (a) convinced that there is no viable alternative, and (b) prepared to take strong action to support any developing countries that might be adversely affected by any new trade restrictions that may be required. Free trade is certainly good for business, and it appears to be good for the poor countries of the world, where wages are low and conditions poor.

My colleague, Hugh Lacey,[22] has commented:

> As I look at recent history in Brazil, there is some truth in this—once poor people have been removed from the land and pushed into slums, and into doing work for little pay and under terrible conditions, free trade does contribute to bettering the lives of large numbers of them.

But he goes on to say that 'for many of them, being pushed into these conditions in the first place was itself a consequence of free trade practices—it involved an impoverishment of their lives, and the elimination of the hope that they had for their lives, based in improving forms of agriculture'.

This may well be so. But the sub-policy of exporting our manufacturing, packing and assembly industries to third world countries was not *inherently* bad for them. Its ill effects in Brazil were due to the exploitation of rural people by home-grown capitalists, not the ill effects of globalization. But it is true that globalization is not always a boon to the developing world. Sometimes it presages even more exploitation.

Be that as it may, globalization is certainly against the interests of the unskilled and blue-collar workers of the rich world. It puts many of them out of a job, and does nothing to help them find a new one. And, this is a consequence that globalization is directly responsible for. It has stripped these workers in the rich world of nearly all of the benefits their ancestors struggled so hard, for so many years, to achieve through their union activity, and forced them to accept lower wages, and much poorer working conditions, than they would otherwise have had.

But restrictive trade practices cannot now be imposed without great risk of bad economic consequences, not to mention the possibility of economic sanctions. There would appear to be only one practical way to proceed, if we want to create full employment for, and restore the dignity of, Australia's currently under-employed working class. We must return to the tried and true policies that led to the establishment of the post-war welfare state in Australia, and its further development under Gough Whitlam, and take it from there into the present century.

Part III

Targeted Development

The case for replacing *laissez faire* development with *targeted* development was made in Part II, where it was argued there that a neoliberal society does not, and probably cannot, produce enough work of the kinds required to allow everyone who wants a suitable job can find one. But a good society requires an environment in which everyone can live with dignity, develop their capacities and interests, and participate fully in the life of the community to which they belong. In a capitalist society, this requires that everyone should be able to find a suitable job in their own community. For they have to be able to pay their way. There is, therefore, a fundamental tension within capitalism. Capitalist economic progress is not the same as social progress. Therefore, any society that seeks to employ the capitalist business model of creative destruction described by Joseph Schumpeter (1975/1942), must face up to the fact that *laissez faire* development is just not good enough.

But *laissez faire* development is very good at the frontier of developing new products and processes. It is even better if the entrepreneurs, who are the frontline developers, are up to date with the latest technologies and their scientific foundations. So, any country that wants to use the neoliberal model, must provide a first class scientific or technological education for its entrepreneurs.[23] It must also make sure that the whole community is scientifically well-informed. For governments need to know what developments might occur, and what their consequences might be, so that they can impose reasonable social, geographical, or global constraints upon them.

But, to be successful socially, the education of entrepreneurs cannot be the only target for development that the state must promote. For, as we have argued in Part I, the society has a social front to develop as well—one that must be much more reactive to what is going on in the communities that the nation must serve.[24] The social service ministry must try to understand the social problems that people have in these communities, and provide whatever services may be necessary for dealing with them. Technology may have a role to play in this process, and in the area of modern communications, possibly even a major role. But it is unlikely to be a role that goes much beyond helping people use their communications equipment. And this is not a task that is at all like that of the entrepreneurs who want to develop them. It is the sort of job that most young people, who have been brought up with this equipment, can do easily.

Social services inevitably require professional people trained in psychology, drug addiction, rehabilitation, sociology, social work, medicine, legal aid services, teachers, and in many other fields, who can live or work in the communities that need assistance, and supervise any care or treatment facilities that may have to be provided. But much of the work involved in the provision of care and treatment will naturally be the sort of work that most adults can do, and have been doing all their lives. For it involves a lot of work that is pretty much on a par with that of helping to assist mature-aged people in their own homes—people who are getting old, have fallen out of the workforce, or are being overwhelmed by the pace of change.

Between them, these two fronts of development should provide enough work for the workforces of most societies, catering to the needs of both skilled and unskilled workers, and distributing work opportunities widely throughout the communities that need social support services.

3.1. Internet Technology

It should be no surprise that I begin with IT as the first area for targeted development. It is often said that governments should not be in the game of picking winners. True. But they must be in the game of picking the races to compete in. If we don't enter the industrial races for fear of failure, we will never win one. As a society, we have to behave like Bart Cummings, who trained 11 Melbourne Cup winners. And Australia should be well and truly in the game of training winners. While one cannot be sure which projects are going to pay off, one can be sure about which ones will not. If Flashing Sally is a cow, there is no chance at all that she will win the Melbourne Cup. Likewise, we know that the old technology of the 20th century will play a much smaller role in this one, and that its place will be taken by intelligent machines, rather than by machines that must rely upon human intelligence to manage and guide them. We also know that the old carbon-based technologies are on their way out, and a sensible trainer will not be listening to pundits who think that coal and oil have a bright future.

To develop this whole area, we, as a nation, must invest heavily in IT start-up companies. But, while governments may encourage this development, sow the seeds of it through technical education, and invest in IT research and development centres, they should not, as the old saying goes, be picking winners. IT research teams will have no option but to compete on the open market for start-up capital. But fairness, like justice, should not only exist in our practise, it should appear to do so, and for governments to do the selecting would be an open invitation to corruption. For millions, even billions, of dollars could be at stake.

3.2. Immigrants and Refugees

Instability in the Middle East has created the most serious refugee crisis since the Second World War. Morally, we must offer refuge to them, and undertake to resettle as many as we can of those who have no realistic prospect of returning to their homelands. As members of the Coalition of the Willing, we began this dreadful series of wars in the Middle East by invading Iraq. We are not responsible for all of the hostilities in the Middle East today, but we were certainly among the initiators of the deadly conflict, which has raged in this region ever since. Moreover, our moral obligation does not only derive from this. It derives also from our status as a wealthy immigrant nation, and the appalling circumstances in which these people now find themselves.

Australia could, in fact, benefit from extending a helping hand to refugees from the Middle East, just as it undoubtedly did by accommodating European refugees in the circumstances that existed just after the Second World War. Many of the post-war immigrants were young and talented, and the work of post-depression reconstruction provided employment for everyone for the next thirty years. Australia is, as I have argued, now in a situation that is not unlike the one that existed back then. We have not kept up with modern internet technology, we have allowed our STEM teaching and research to become second rate, and we have deliberately prolonged our heavy dependence upon extractive and carbon-intensive industries. Moreover, if Steven Keen and Satyajit Das are right, and we are already in the early stages of a post-GFC Depression—which seems likely to be at least as prolonged as the one in the 1930s—we will need all of the work that we can create to employ our people, and all of the talent and strength of the Middle Eastern immigrants to help us do the work.

If these diagnoses are correct, then Australia must now throw its weight behind remaking itself as a progressive and technically savvy social democracy that is committed to a strongly egalitarian philosophy, and to building a nation that is shaped by the *Universal Declaration of Human Rights,* and committed to upholding the social, economic and cultural rights of that great document.

3.3. Social Services

The area of development that has been most neglected in the neoliberal era is, naturally, that of social services. People living in wealthy suburbs may find this hard to believe, because mostly they are well-cared for themselves. But the same is not the case everywhere. People living in poor suburbs or declining country towns are likely to be most in need, and ultimately to be the greatest users of social services. For, in a society in which 'user pays' is the accepted rule, social services are likely to suffer most in the suburbs and townships where their need is greatest. Therefore, in a socially egalitarian society, the needs of the poorest sections of the community must take priority. Such areas must inevitably draw more heavily on the public purse than others. Consequently, a state of the kind we need for the present century must have a large and competent civil service—one that is adequate to administer and develop the society's extensive social amenities.

We should aim to include at least the following on our list of social services (which I here arrange in random order):

1. *home care for the elderly*: to support people for as long as possible in their own homes,

2. *disability support services*: to enable disabled people to live normal lives of their own choosing,

3. *drug treatment and rehabilitation centres*: to provide ready access to professional services in suburbs and townships throughout the nation,

4. *women's refuges and support services*: to be made readily available to women everywhere,

5. *child care services*: including preschool education,

6. *technical support services*: to help people adapt to and cope with rapidly changing technology in their own homes,

7. *aboriginal welfare and development*: to provide support for aboriginal communities to create good and productive lives for their members in their chosen environments,

8. *immigrant and refugee support*: to assist with problems of language, culture, and living in their new country,

9. *continuing education and training*: to provide opportunities to learn new skills, and to become better adapted to the requirements of employers,

10. *secular moral education and cultural development*: to engage people in secular philosophical discussions of social, moral, political, and cultural issues about life in Australia,

11. *gardening and household maintenance*: to assist in garden and household maintenance for the elderly and disabled,

12. *social housing*: to provide, supervise and administer units of social housing to ensure that no one needs to sleep rough anywhere in Australia,

13. *counseling and psychiatric services*: the idea here is that there should be professional community psychologists and social workers readily accessible for support and guidance in the towns and suburbs of the nation,

14. *seasonal provision of holiday services*: to provide, supply, and attend to kiosks, cafés, coffee shops, and other facilities in holiday or tourist venues according to seasonal demand,

15. *forest and woodlands maintenance*: to provide and attend to walking tracks, recreation and camping areas in appropriate places,

16. *animal refuges and rescue services*: to provide and maintain these services,

17. *pet care, grooming, and dog-walking*: to assist with the

> care, maintenance and exercise of pets in the homes of the elderly and infirm.

Many, if not all, of these services are readily available in the wealthier suburbs of the big cities. But governments have to ensure that they are available, and also affordable, for the people living in the poorer suburbs, devastated by unemployment, and in remote country towns, where there is little in the public purse to spend on such things.

I imagine that most of these services should be administered by local governments from social service centres located in all of the significant towns and suburbs of the nation, and funded according to the needs of the areas they are required to serve.

The good thing about this largely unmet demand for social services is that it is widespread, and concentrated in areas in which shortages of employment opportunities are greatest. Therefore, in seeking to address the deficiency in social services provision, we shall also be addressing the problem of providing adequate employment for people of the kinds they are able to do, and work in the areas in which they mostly live.

These services would naturally have to be heavily subsidised, but it should not be beyond the resources of State and Federal governments to provide the required support. For the provision of these services will immediately provide paid work in suburbs and country towns everywhere, and where it is most urgently needed. It should also (a) yield more government revenue through increased taxation (b) reduce demand on unemployment services, and (c) increase demands for social workers, social administrators, detoxification specialists, psychiatrists, and others who specialise in drug rehabilitation, obesity, low self-esteem,

91

or any of the other social diseases of the neoliberal era. And, all of these changes should have knock-on effects that will naturally benefit other businesses in these badly affected areas.

The changes would also eliminate the need for that dreadful practice of making unemployed people apply for dozens, or even hundreds, of jobs they do not want, and have little hope of getting, just to keep up appearances. This grotesque practice exists, I surmise, (a) to reduce the length of the unemployment queues, and (b) to prove to a gullible public that if the unemployed cannot find suitable work, then it is really all their own fault.

3.4. Clean Energy

It is clear that we should now be training a whole army of people competent in the various fields of low-carbon technology. For, this is where much future employment must lie. Therefore, any sensible government should be steering students into these fields. But our previous neoliberal government (that of Tony Abbott) was not even a sensible one. Its lack of intelligence was not, however, a fault of neoliberalism. Opposition to clean energy technologies appears to be a disease of countries that are unusually rich in coal or oil shales—Australia and Canada, for example. But the conservative cores of the neoliberal establishments of many other countries appear to be more willing to tackle the problems posed by global warming by attacking its causes.

It is perhaps symptomatic of the problem we face here that there was no science minister in the Abbott government. Moreover, there was no special focus on STEM subjects (science, technology, engineering and mathematics) in our schools. In fact, education generally, and technical education in particular, were, it seems, sabotaged by the Howard government's ideological promotion of private education at the expense of public. For our state schools have always been highly productive of scientists, engineers, and technologists, who, as I have argued in *Rationalism* (forthcoming), are the real generators of the wealth of nations—and have been, at least since the eighteenth century. The anti-science stance of the recently past neoliberal government has left the country dangerously out of touch with current technical developments.

Strictly speaking, there is no good reason why this anti-science stance should have been taken. It does not follow from the argument for remaking society in the image of a neoclassical perfect market. For, there is no reason why the residents of a perfect market should avoid research and development in science and technology, or in any other area. On the contrary, if you really believed that specialisation, and the division of labour in the production of goods and services, were the sources of all wealth, you should also give some thought as to why people should want to buy the things they produce. And, basically, people want to buy things, not because they are being offered for sale, or because they are cheap, but because they are technically better, or better designed, than other similarly priced things on offer. Therefore, you should also be in favour of developing technically better things, designing them better, and promoting the learning facilities that produce the people who can achieve these results.

Another reason, which may resonate with some economists, is the idea that businessmen are the real drivers of economic growth—not scientists, technicians, designers, or other creative people who make things, but the business people who invest their money in them. They are the 'lifters', they say, who do the hard work of developing the economy. But, as I have argued elsewhere (Ellis, 2015), science and technology are the true sources of economic growth; business people are the ones who make money out of them. Scientists and technologists are not the meek servants of industry, even if some of them are employed by industry. They are the creative ones, who are the real forces behind industrial development and growth. And, they are the ones who have powered all of the industrial revolutions in history, and the ones who will assuredly power the next one.

But, instead of urging entrepreneurs and researchers to develop clean energy technologies for Australia, so that we could be ahead of the game, the Abbott government did all it could to hinder developments in this area. Consequently, important business opportunities were almost certainly lost. We could, for example, have developed wind-, wave- and solar- power technologies, while the opportunities were still there, and sold them on to the world. But instead we chose to pretend that anthropogenic global warming was not happening. Future governments, whatever their colour, will still have to invest heavily in low-carbon technologies. But the chances are that we have already lost the golden opportunity we had in the eighties and nineties, when it first became evident to most scientists that global warming would probably occur as a result of carbon pollution.

3.5. How is it All to be Paid For?

In *Labor's Historic Mission,* I said that I had not asked, and did not intend to try, to answer this question. I said that the job of a political philosopher is to ask the right questions, as Tony Judt so strongly urged upon us. And I think that this is what I have been trying to do here. But, I also said that it is not my job to say what should be included in the state of targeted full employment, which I think should be our aim for the 21st century, or how it should be paid for. Indeed, I said:

> It is the job of political philosophers to try to answer the basic questions concerning what we should be aiming to do. It is the job of economists to keep an eye on costs, and advise governments on how best to do what they want to do, given their objectives. Then, it is the job of politicians, who, having fixed upon their overall agenda, to determine their priorities, develop practical policies, determine what the pace of change should be, and put their programme to the electorate for endorsement.

I then went on to say:

> Economists have to be relegated to the footnotes, where they belong. In the thirty or so years since the neoliberal era began, nineteenth century economic rationalists have been allowed to set the political agenda in Australia, and have been given centre stage in the political debate. But this is fundamentally wrong. The questions we should be asking are: What do we want to achieve? What is achievable? What are our priorities? How should we go about trying to implement the policies we think are best? Clearly, we shall need economic advice in trying to answer these questions. And, we should be seeking the best economic advice that we can get from academic economists. But I do not advocate populism. Our trusted advisors must be people who understand the price of inequality, and the dangers of capitalism in the 21st century.

That is, they must be new cutting-edge economists of the 21st century, not the old ones who hanker after the 'certainties' of the early 20th century.[25] They must be economists who are fully aware of the difficulties faced by rich nations that seek to achieve accelerating growth as a means of dealing with high unemployment.

But, we have to relax a bit, and allow the government to decide on behalf of the people they represent, what *social* goods or services are required, and employ, or subsidise the employment of, the people to provide them. And we must strive to suppress the kneejerk response of all neoliberals to ask: Where is the money coming from? Obviously, it has to come mostly from people who can afford to pay it. But to even ask the question is to misunderstand the position. For our obligation to provide adequately for a social demand of this kind is not an optional extra. It is moral obligation. It is a moral requirement on government, because every society, with a standard of living like ours, is similarly obliged. And, a universalisable social obligation of this kind is not just an option; it is moral commitment.

I am sympathetic to the idea that those who have invested heavily in neoliberal perks in the past, should not be punished for doing so. They were just doing what the neoliberal government of the time encouraged them to do. But nor should they be allowed to stand in the way of those who want to reform the system to remove these perks. If governments were only honest about what they have done, and what they are now doing, and why they did what they did, and we had a public forum that would allow careful examination of proposals, we might be able to silence the strident abuse that is likely to be heaped upon the reformers.

But our conservative neoliberal core of voters, interviewers, journalists, and tweeters, will naturally be very unhappy with this response. It goes against just about everything they have learnt since the neoliberal era began. Where's the money coming from to do all of these things? That is the question that nearly everyone will ask, and nearly everyone will insist that philosophers like me should answer it. 'Put up or shut up' is what they would say.

But why should people who think about the basic questions, and suggest proper answers, have to 'put up or shut up'? Isn't that what Tony Judt was complaining about? In Part I of this paper, it was argued that social demand is not directly comparable to economic demand. Its value is social not economic. Economic demand is easily measured. So, one can always make a business case for choosing a cheaper option, if economic demands are the only relevant variables. But one cannot make a business case for satisfying a social demand at the expense of an economic one, because social demands are not quantifiable, and so essentially incomparable. The good that is being sought is not a marketable good, and so it does not have a calculable economic value. But social demands, like getting a well-paid job, or a decent education, are real and important, as I have argued at length in Part I. And, making informed decisions concerning their satisfaction is the basic nature of social democratic decision-making. The questioner is out of order, I want to say, because he or she is demanding a business case where no business case is possible. The only relevant question is whether the overall social demand would be better satisfied by some alternative social policy.

The idea that those who cannot say where the money is coming from are not to be trusted, and should not therefore be listened to, is not a theoretically neutral one. It is, in fact, a basic thesis of neoliberalism that all decisions should be made, as though they were business decisions. It is fair enough to demand a business case for decisions between competing economic demands. But Australia is not an enterprise *within* a state. It is a state. And, as a state, it has prior moral obligations to its citizens. So, the first thing we have to look for is not a business case for a development, but a social or moral one for immediate action.

It is true that no business person would engage upon a major reform program of the kind I am here advocating here, without having a business case to show that it is economically optimal. But my point is that there cannot be a business case for a program of radical reform, which would effectively bury a neoliberal view of the state itself. There can be a moral case, however. And there can be a well-argued meta-theory that neoliberalism has failed us as a political philosophy, and needs to be replaced by a radical alternative. And this essay should be considered to be such a meta-theory.

The radical alternative that I am proposing is not really new. It is a reversion to the kind of political philosophy that generated the welfare states of the post-war period. And, I am suggesting only that we should seek to build a moral society, and go about it in the kind of way that Chifley, Menzies and Whitlam would have gone about it. That is, we should set our goals out first, according to our consciences, and then, having decided on moral grounds what we should try to do if we can, set about creating programs to achieve our goals in the most economic and rational way we can.

3.6. Directed Growth

I began writing this essay with a view to justifying the aim of achieving a low growth economy in a wealthy nation such as ours. But I do not think that the argument I have presented leads to this conclusion. It leads only to the

conclusion that the active pursuit of strong growth is dangerous, and, if successful, likely to lead to possibly disastrous economic instability.

I argued that a neoliberal state such as ours, which must demand high levels of economic growth if it is to fulfil its moral obligations, needs to be replaced by a sort of welfare state, which does not promise high growth, but is strongly committed to providing a wide range of employment opportunities for everyone who wishes to work, and a prosperous society, in which people can actively pursue any of the different kinds of activity that they might reasonably wish for in their lives. Such a state might, or might not, be one with high levels of economic growth. It must be prosperous, but economic growth is not a measure of prosperity. If a society's growth is properly targeted, it could easily supply plenty of everything for everyone, as well as first rate personal and social services. And, our efforts as a nation should be to achieve high levels of such genuine prosperity.

A prosperous state is one in which nearly everyone is able to prosper in their own way. I suppose that everyone would have his or her own conception of what they would wish for in their society. But a market society, such as ours, can easily supply all of the goods and services needed to fulfil most people's wishes.

The key to prosperity in an economically neoliberal state is paid employment. If everyone who wants or needs to work can find adequate and satisfying work, and everyone is paid sufficiently for what they do, then the society will be prosperous by most standards. The trouble with neoliberal societies that do not target growth and development is simply that they cannot provide enough work for people to do, at least not without creating a society in which everyone is burdened with unsustainable levels of debt, which threaten the society's stability.

So, what we must now do to create full employment is go outside the market to create jobs for everyone, wherever they may live. Specifically, we must put people to work in social and personal services, which exist everywhere, and which may need to be subsidised by the state. For these are the areas that have been systematically neglected during the neoliberal era, and whose development should provide a foundation for a new welfare state. To realise this dream, we must retrain people whose services have become redundant, due to FTAs, TPPs and the like, invest heavily in science, engineering, technology and mathematics, and train young people to develop technology for the future of our society. We must also seek look after the old, the sick and the disabled, and try to keep people in their own homes, where they have friends and pets, for as long as possible. In other words, we must develop those areas of service to the community, which make living worthwhile.

REFERENCES

Bell, S. (1997): *Ungoverning the Economy.* Melbourne; Oxford University Press.

Cogwill, M. (2013): *A Shrinking Slice of the Pie.* ACTU; Working Australia Paper, No. 1

Collins, H. (1985): 'Political Ideology in Australia: The Distinctiveness of a Benthamite Society', in S. Graubard (ed.) *Australia: The Daedalus Symposium,* (published in 1985 as an issue of *Daedalus*). Melbourne: Angus and Robertson.

Crawford, R. M. (1952): *Australia.* London; Hutchinson's University Library.

Davidson, P. (2009): *John Maynard Keynes.* In *Great Thinkers in Economics*, Series Editor: A. P. Thirwell. Basingstoke, U.K.; Palgrave Macmillan.

Ellis, B. D. (2012): *Social Humanism: A New Metaphysics.* New York and London; Routledge.

Ellis, B. D. (2015): *Labor's Historic Mission.* Melbourne; Australian Scholarly Publishing.

Ellis, B. D. (forthcoming): *Rationalism: A Critique of Pure Theory.* Melbourne; Australian Scholarly Publishing.

Faulkner, J. (2008): 'In the Tradition of Pragmatic Idealism.' Speech to launch Ashley Hogan's book, Edgecliff Sydney. <http://evatt/org.au/papers>

Fisher, I. (1933): 'The Debt-deflation Theory of Great Depressions', *Econometrica* 1: 337-355.

Fraser, M., with Roberts, C. (2014): *Dangerous Allies.* Melbourne; Melbourne University Press.

Gleeson-White, J. (2014): *Six Capitals: The Revolution Capitalism has to have—or Can Accountants Save the Planet?* London; Allen and Unwin.

Glover, D. (2015): *An Economy is not a Society: Winners and Losers in the New Australia.* Melbourne; Black Inc. Publishing, Redback Series.

Helévy, E. (1972): *The Growth of Philosophic Radicalism.* London; Faber and Faber.

Hogan, A. (2008): *Moving in the Open Daylight; Doc Evatt, an Australian at the United Nations.* Sydney; Sydney University Press.

Judt, T. (2010): *Ill Fares the Land.* London; Allen Lane.

Keen, S. (2001): *Debunking Economics: The Naked Emperor of the Social Sciences.* London and New York; Zed Books.

Keen, S. (2011): *Debunking Economics: The Naked Emperor of the Social Sciences.* Second Edition. *Revised, Expanded, and Integrated.* London and New York; Zed Books.

Keynes, J. M. (1936/1973): *The General Theory of Employment, Interest and Money.* New York; Harcourt Brace. Reprinted as *The Collected Writings of John Maynard Keynes 7,* edited by D. Moggridge, London, Macmillan

Keynes, J. M. (1937): 'The General Theory of Employment', *Quarterly Journal of Economics* 51: 209-223.

Kirby, M (2008): 'H. V. Evatt and the United Nations; After 60 Years.' H. V. Evatt Lecture 2008.

Kline, N. (2014): *This Changes Everything: Capitalism vs Climate.* London; Allen Lane.

Kuhn, T. (1962): *The Structure of Scientific Revolutions.* Chicago; University of Chicago Press.

Lynch, A. (2012/13): 'The Moral Narrative of Social Democracy', *Dissent* 40, pp. 25-31.

Lynch, A. (forthcoming): 'The Contemporary Development Paradigm: Towards a Critical Understanding of Neoliberal Agency'. Unpublished manuscript.

Metin, A. (1901/1977): *Socialisme sans doctrines*, F. Alcan, translated by Russel Ward as *Socialism without Doctrine.* Chippendale, NSW; Alternative Publishing Cooperative.

Meyer, T., with Hinchman, L. (2007): *The Theory of Social Democracy.* Cambridge UK and Maiden MA; Polity Press. Translated from the German *Theorie der sozialen Democratie* (2005)

Nozick, R. (1974): *Anarchy, State and Utopia* Oxford; Basil Blackwell.

Rawls, J. (1971): *A Theory of Justice.* London; Oxford University Press.

Richardson, D, and Denniss, R. (2014): 'Income and Wealth Inequality in Australia' The Australia Institute, Policy Brief No. 64.

Rosanvallon, P., with Goldhammer, A. (2013): *The Society of Equals.* Translated from the French *Société des* égaux (2011). Cambridge, Mass.; Harvard University Press.

Schumpeter, J. (1975/1942): *Capitalism, Socialism and Democracy.* New York; Harper.

Sen, A. (1993): 'Capability and Well-being', in M. Nussbaum and A. Sen eds. *The Quality of Life*, pp. 30-53.

Spence, A. M. (2011). *The Next Convergence: The Future of Economic Growth in a Multispeed World.* New York: Farrar, Straus and Giroux.

Stiglitz, J. (2012): *The Price of Inequality.* Allan Lane

Walras, L. (1900/1977): *Elements of Pure Economics, or The Theory of Social Wealth*, translated by William Jaffe. Fairfield; Augustus M. Kelley – Publishers.

Internet References

1. Australia's Private Debt

   http://www.smh.com.au/business/the-economy/australian-households-awash-with-debt-barclays-20150316-1lzyz4.html

2. Unemployment in Australia

   Google: Australian Unemployment Rate Graph Images

Notes

1. At least, that is what we are told it is for. But realistically, the greatest threat we face is from insurrection, which is a suppressed fear of the very wealthy in almost every country. It has been lurking at the back of people's minds ever since the French Revolution.

2. Including the USSR, UKSSR (Ukraine), BSSR (Byelorussia), Yugoslavia, Poland, and Czechoslovakia.

3. John Rawls, *A Theory of Justice*, (Belknap Press, 1971). (According to Google Scholar the book has been cited in the academic literature 41, 156 times.)

4. This is the point of Robert Nozick's *Anarchy, State & Utopia*, (New York: Basic Books, 1973).

5. This is what modern democracy means.

6. Ellis, op. cit. p. x

7. Ellis, op. cit. p. 8

8. As I argue at length in Chapter 6 of my book on *Rationalism* (forthcoming), this thesis is almost certainly false. The historical cause of the economic ascendancy of Western civilization in the two hundred years or so since the European Enlightenment began is almost certainly the growth of Western of science and technology in this period.

9. David Richardson and Richard Denniss, 2014.

10. But it was still double average unemployment level (of 2.0%) for the thirty years from 1945 to 1975. Such low levels of unemployment were not rare or unexpected for this period. The French called it 'les trente glorieuses'

11 A dramatic decline in the production, use, addiction to, and treatment of the victims of metamphetamine (ice), would, for example, be an unqualified gain for Australian society. But it would result directly in a loss of productive activity, and therefore a reduction of GDP. It may well be the case that such a reduction would lead to compensating increases in GDP. But a successful program for dealing with the problem of ice and its addictions would be fully justified, whether or not there were any compensating gains of this kind.

12 Ben Chifley's welfare state and the *Universal Declaration of Human Rights*, to which Bert Evatt made a significant contribution, have the same philosophical foundation, viz. a strongly egalitarian form of social humanism. (See *Labor's Historic Mission* (Ellis, 2015))

13 This example has been discussed at length in Keen's (2001 and 2011). To my mind, the example is much more damaging to monetary unrealism than Keynes's original objections to the Neutral Money Hypothesis of neoclassical theory.

14 This may sound reasonable. But I am ignorant here. If Australian banks are the debtors and Chinese banks the creditors, in whose books do these credit and debit entries cancel one another? Intuitively, it does matter. Because if our private banks have lent too much, and had to borrow from China, our government could not just nationalise them and cancel the debt. China would naturally object. And, given that China is a major power in the world, we would be powerless to resist their demands. Interestingly, the American economy is immune to such pressure, and the American economists who dominate their profession have never had to answer this question.

15 And who is to say that such factors are not the cause?

16 The recession of 1991-2 did not become a depression. But the action taken by the Howard Government did not avoid a depression, it only delayed it. That depression is the one that is now in progress.

17 If a government chooses to invite the participation of big business in a public /private partnership, that is one thing. But no international agreement *between governments* should make

any government vulnerable to being sued by a corporation.

18 I use the phrase 'real equality of opportunity' in the way defined in (Ellis, 2012). It implies having the capacity to act on the opportunity presented. Hence, real equality may require providing education or training, not just making legal provision for it.

19 At least, the neoliberal era should by now be over. But there may be some surviving pockets of neoliberalism, and given Australia's recent history of burying its head in the sand over climate change, there can be no assurance that the Australian chapter is over quite yet.

20 Debt deflation is the mechanism postulated by Irving Fisher (1933) as the driver of the Great Depression.

21 Australians could not live with dignity in Australia, as Australian citizens, on the wages that the workers in India or China are paid. And, it would be quite unrealistic to expect them to do so.

22 Scheuer Family Professor of Philosophy Emeritus at Swarthmore College, USA, and an Adjunct Professor of the Institute of Advanced Studies at the University of Sao Paulo, Brazil.

23 In my view, the Business Schools of Australia should seek to engage more students with degrees in science, technology, engineering or mathematics, (STEM subjects) or advanced technical diplomas, or their equivalents, in IT subjects. But see also footnote 17.

24 So, our Business Schools should not limit their intakes those educated in the STEM subjects. We need university and technical graduates of all kinds to be involved in business administration. Business administration and development is too important to be left to businessmen and businesswomen.

25 The names of Steven Keen and Satyajit Das come to mind. For they, at least, seem to understand how the world has been changed by the explosive growth that was created in the neoliberal era.

www.ingramcontent.com/pod-product-compliance
Ingram Content Group Australia Pty Ltd
76 Discovery Rd, Dandenong South VIC 3175, AU
AUHW020841060325
407965AU00004B/33